# SECRET CITY
## *HIDDEN HISTORY OF ST ALBANS*

James Corbett

McDERMOTT MARKETING

Published by McDermott Marketing
St Albans, 0727 846862

© James Corbett 1993

ISBN 0 9522664 0 7

British Cataloguing-in-Publication Data.
A catalogue record for this book is available from the British Library

All rights reserved. No part of this book may be reproduced in any form or by any means, without permission from the publisher.

Published in conjunction with
St Albans City and District Council

Printed by Dodimead Ball Ltd., St Albans

# CONTENTS

| | | |
|---|---|---|
| | Illustrations | i |
| | Acknowledgements | iv |
| | FAME IS LIKE A RIVER<br>Introduction | 1 |
| 1 | UNDAUNTED COURAGE<br>Alban Roe | 3 |
| 2 | GRIPING LANDLORDS DO TAKE ADVANTAGE<br>Tithes | 10 |
| 3 | WHO WOULD TRUE VALOUR SEE<br>John Townsend | 16 |
| 4 | THE KIND PHYSICIAN<br>Nathaniel Cotton | 23 |
| 5 | ABUNDANT CAUSE TO REMEMBER<br>Isabella Worley | 30 |
| 6 | SIGN OF THE TIMES<br>*The Garibaldi* | 38 |
| 7 | KEPT BACK BY FRAUD<br>Farmworkers | 45 |
| 8 | THE BATTLE OF SANDPIT LANE<br>Enclosure | 53 |
| 9 | THAT VIRULENT DISEASE<br>Smallpox | 62 |
| 10 | FESTIVAL OF HISTORY<br>1381 – 1981 | 68 |
| | Sources | 75 |
| | Index | 77 |

# ILLUSTRATIONS

1. Francis Bacon: a memorial statue in St Michael's Church, St Albans.
2. St Albans, 1634. *(St Albans Central Library)*
3. Alban Roe outside St Albans Abbey gateway in a stained glass window at the Church of Our Lady of Lourdes, Harpenden.
4. A plaque on a traffic island at the junction of Edgware Road and Bayswater Road, London, marks the site of Tyburn gallows.
5. Alban Roe's mortuary bill, dated 8 February 1642, records his death. *(Douai Abbey, Reading)*
6. The Royal Mail issued four postage stamps in June 1992 to commemorate the outbreak of the Civil War in 1642. The stamps show soldiers from the opposing armies. *(Reproduced by permission of Royal Mail)*
7. Robert Morden's map of Hertfordshire, 1704. *(Herts County Record Office)*
8. The Civil War made life harder for farmers.
9. Part of a Dutch woodcut, 1653, shows Oliver Cromwell seated in council.
10. St Peter's Church, St Albans, before its nineteenth century restoration.
11. The passage through St Albans Abbey Church. *(St Albans Central Library)*
12. Sir Harbottle Grimston. *(National Portrait Gallery)*
13. A tract published in 1662 denounced the trial proceedings following the death of John Townsend. *(St Albans Central Library)*
14. Rev William Haworth is commemorated in the vestibule of what is now the United Reformed Church, Hertford.
15. Nathaniel Cotton. *(St Albans and Hertfordshire Architectural and Archaeological Society)*

16  Title-page of Nathaniel Cotton's most popular work. *(St Albans Central Library)*

17  Collegium Insanorum. *(St Albans Central Library)*

18  William Cowper in the garden with his pets.

19  Sopwell House, 1993.

20  Christ Church, St Albans, 1858. *(Herts Advertiser)*

21  The Wooden Room, St Albans, 1993.

22  Mrs Worley's fountain in Victoria Square, St Albans, 1993.

23  A general election advertisement in the Herts Advertiser of 21 November 1885 groups Lattimore with Cobden and Bright. *(St Albans Central Library)*

24  'The old Garibaldi Tavern', by Holmes Winter, 1898. *(St Albans Central Library)*

25  Garibaldi's portrait was returned to *The Garibaldi* in 1991. Flanking Alice Brown, the donor, and Richard Fuller, a director of Fuller's Brewery, are the public house's manageress, Anna Quick, and manager, Paul McFarlane. *(St Albans & Harpenden Observer)*

26  A farm worker wearing 'that ancient and pictureque garment', a smock.

27  Joseph Arch.

28  Canon Owen Davys. *(St Albans Central Library)*

29  A collector's indoor fern piller, 1869.

30  An Ordnance Survey map of 1898 shows the common land on the south side of Sandpit Lane. *(St Albans Central Library)*

31  William Hurlock. (St Albans Central Library)

32  Comrades in arms: memorial stones were laid at the Baptist Tabernacle, Victoria Street, St Albans, by William Hurlock and (33) Henry Taylor.

34  Sir Edmund Beckett (Lord Grimthorpe). *(St Albans Central Library)*

35  'Brummagem Joe' Chamberlain.

36 Date plaque - A.D. 1902 - on the front wall of terrace houses in Cannon Street, St Albans.

37 Lady Mary Wortley Montagu.

38 Arthur Ekins. *(The Museum of St Albans)*

39 The Sisters' Hospital, 1893, is now part of St Albans City Hospital.

40 Deirdre Roger's poster traces the causes and course of the Peasants' Revolt in St Albans.

41 Edwin Hudson.

42 A commemorative pottery mug made in St Albans.

43 Young Liberals march with the agricultural workers and others along St Peter's Street, St Albans.

44 The marchers were led by Jack Boddy, general secretary of the National Union of Agricultural and Allied Workers, Joan Maynard M.P., and Norman Willis, deputy general secretary of the Trades Union Congress. *(St Albans Review)*

45 Farmworkers' badge.

# ACKNOWLEDGMENTS

IN the first place my thanks are due to Sheila Bond, who proposed *Secret City* as a course for the WEA, and to the students for their patient encouragement and illuminating comments; to William Bond for his generous contribution of slides and photographs, and to Mary Willson and Jeremy White for their constructive criticisms of the consequent typescript: the latter reader also kindly made available his translation from the Latin of Alban Roe's mortuary bill.

For information and assistance I am especially grateful to Reg Auckland, Alice Brown, Marjorie Byers, Robin and Val Corbett, John Cox, Vincent and Pam Forster, Elisabeth Goffe, Elisabeth Hudson, Paul McFarlane, Barrie Morley, Alan Norris, Kerry Pollard, Neville and Trudi Postlethwaite, Anna Quick, Deirdre Rogers, Dom Geoffrey Scott OSB, Margaret Taylor, Maggie Telfer, Marjorie Webb and Joyce Wells, librarian and archivist of the St Albans and Hertfordshire Architectural and Archaeological Society.

The Very Rev Canon Maurice O'Leary, of the Church of Our Lady of Lourdes, Harpenden, and the Rev Jeanne Ennals, of the United Reformed Church, Hertford, readily gave permission for photographs to be taken inside their respective places of worship. The illustrations listed without a provenance are from some of the kind individuals acknowledged above or from the author's collection.

I am indebted to the staffs of The British Library, Buckinghamshire Record Office, Hertfordshire Central Resources Library, Hertfordshire County Record Office, The Museum of St Albans and St Albans Central Library: all were at all times attentive and tireless. Messrs Fuller Smith and Turner plc were singularly helpful concerning *The Garibaldi* public house. And for their generous assistance it would be unforgivable not to thank Patrick McDermott, of McDermott Marketing, and Roger Osborn, public relations officer of the City and District of St Albans. Mary, my wife, gave her usual unfailing and informed support. The errors are my own.

# FAME IS LIKE A RIVER

*Certainly, fame is like a river, that beareth up things light and swoln, and drowns things weighty and solid.*

Francis Bacon: Of Praise

ST ALBANS has a secret past. It hides notable individuals and remarkable events dating from distant to recent years. Some of them — people and events alike — have been ignored completely; others have been neglected rather than hidden and their claim to fame overlooked. But what caused the secrecy?

Forgetfulness is a possibility. Memory fails. Records are lost. A parish register belonging to the post-Dissolution Abbey Church of St Albans was reported as having been burnt in 1743 but was discovered, more than a hundred years later, under a heap of rubbish in a stable loft in the town.

1. *Francis Bacon: a memorial statue in St Michael's Church, St Albans*

There is another explanation. A picturesque place like St Albans tended to generate picturesque histories. In them, historical facts, having been deemed worthy of retention, were marshalled into a decorous order. Unacceptable facts disappeared from view; other unacceptable facts, too prominent to be avoided, were modified. For example, the uprising of 1381, known to its participants as the Great Fellowship, was designated by Victorians as the 'Peasants' Revolt'. It was a reassuring characterisation: there were no longer any peasants; there would not be any more revolts. The 'prosperous future' of St Albans, confidently forecast by Frederick Mason in his *Illustrated History* of 1884 was safe. Why let awkward aspects of the past spoil the show? And, indeed, the past began to be presented as an elegant pageant.

Nevertheless, important events had recurred which did not always find a place in the history books. The rehabilitation of a representative selection, along with that of the subsequently neglected men and women involved, is the purpose of this investigation.

# 1
# UNDAUNTED COURAGE

*Every one hath it not in that full measure, nor in so audacious and resolute a temper, as to endure those terrible tests and trials . . .*
            Thomas Browne: *Religio Medici*

BARTHOLOMEW Roe died as a consequence of what happened to him in St Albans. It was an awesome happening. He changed his beliefs. He changed his name. Posthumously, because of the manner in which he met a terrible death, his status was changed.

Born in 1583, he was raised a devout Protestant. The English Reformation, initiated by Henry VIII more than fifty years earlier, had transformed the kingdom: Catholicism was banned, attendance at Anglican services was compulsory. In St Albans, the ruins of a magnificent Benedictine abbey were crumbling reminders of the change. Except for the abbey's great gateway, which was being used as a prison, and the abbey's church, bought by townsfolk for use as their parish church, few of the monastic buildings had escaped destruction. The tiny town clustered around St Peter's Street, Holywell Hill and Fishpool Street. Roe might have worshipped in the abbey church; in any case, he would have seen the adjacent ruins.

His parents, who are believed to have lived at Bury St Edmunds, Suffolk, sent him to Cambridge University. While a student he visited St Albans. It is not known why. At the time, a 'mechanic', whose name tantalisingly is recorded simply as 'David', was imprisoned in the gateway for stubborn adherence to the old religion. Roe, an ardent young man, decided to convert him, entered the prison as a visitor and began to argue with David.

4     *UNDAUNTED COURAGE*

The outcome would cost Roe his life. David, a contemptible prisoner, 'slew' the clever, college Goliath: Roe himself was converted. It was a generous response, typical of his impulsive nature but, in those days, perilous. Catholics faced severe penalties. Absence from a Church of England service every Sunday could result in a fine or, for men stubborn as David, imprisonment. And the celebration of Mass constituted a serious crime. On the other hand, when James I ascended the English throne in 1603 he brought with him Anne of Denmark as queen: she also had converted to Catholicism. Perhaps that was a hopeful sign? All the same, Roe was committed: his life would be dedicated to the Catholic cause.

In 1607 he crossed the Channel to the Spanish Netherlands. There, twenty miles south of Lille, at Douai, a seminary founded by English exiles during the previous century, he was accepted for training as a priest. While there, he adopted various

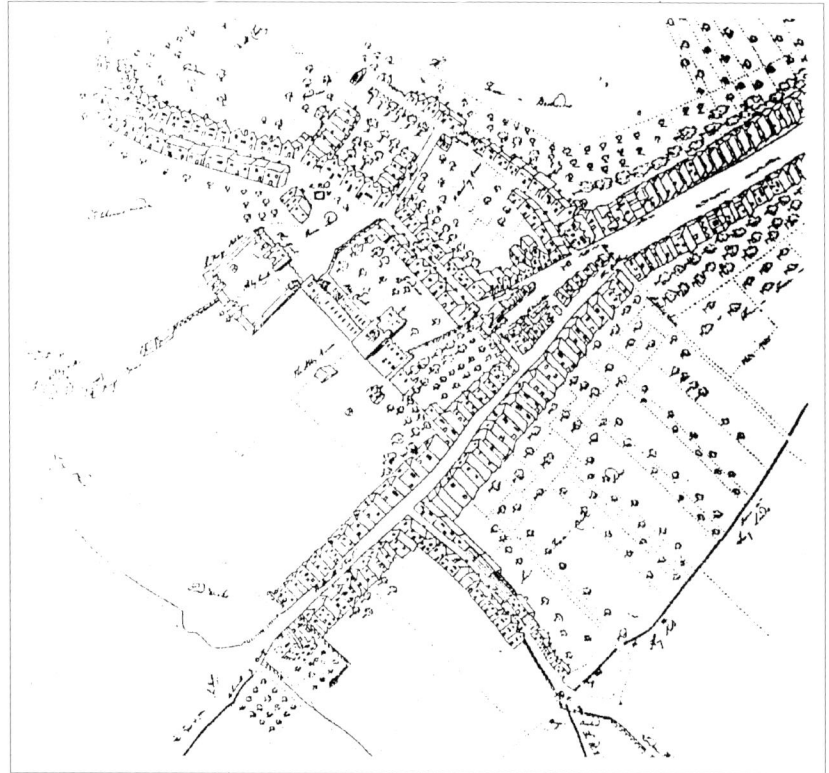

2. *St Albans, 1634*

aliases in a prudent attempt to deflect unwelcome enquiries. Coincidentally, one of the surnames he used, Rolfe, was that of a family well known in St Albans. But Roe's impulsiveness and high spirits got him into trouble: he was dismissed for indiscipline. Undeterred, he made his way eastwards to distant Lorraine where, at the English Benedictine community of St Laurence, Dieulouard, he behaved himself long enough to be professed, in 1614, as a monk, and was ordained. His links with St Albans were further strengthened. Remembering with affection the place of his conversion — the abbey's great gateway — and because of an appropriate devotion to St Alban, the first British martyr, Roe took as his name in religion that of Alban: henceforward he would be called Alban Roe.

Alban Roe returned to England. His happiness at being home, his readiness to face danger, his eagerness, would have been radiantly clear, as was his exuberance. Soon, sedate members of his flock in London, where his ministry had started, were complaining about his lively behaviour. They need not have bothered. Roe, apprehended in 1618 as a fugitive priest, was hurried away to the New prison, near Charing Cross. After five years, banishment followed, thanks to the intervention of the Spanish ambassador, Count Gondomar. Roe chose to go to a newly-established Benedictine priory at Douai but around 1625 resumed his work in England.

That year, James I had died, and was succeeded by his twenty-four-year-old son, Charles I. He, shortly after acceding in March, married Henrietta Maria of France who, like his mother, was a Catholic. Understandably, the young king favoured religious tolerance but had inherited a bloody legacy of repression, retaliation and reprisal. Fundamental was a continuing struggle between the monarchy and Parliament over which should wield executive power. The House of Commons was dominated by austere Protestants, Puritans, who had close links with a City of London opposed to royal interference, and they used persecution tactically: an attack on Catholics was a blow against the autocratic king. Blows fell rapidly. Charles was compelled to expel the French priests in the entourage of Henrietta Maria. Two years later, in 1628, the House of Commons called for a stricter enforcement of the penal laws against Catholics. The call was repeated in the following year, but the king, listening no longer, ignored the call and dissolved his irksome Parliament.

The dissolution prolonged Roe's life. He had returned to St Albans in 1627 perhaps to renew acquaintance with David or to pray at the site of his namesake's shrine in the church of the former abbey. He was caught. Again he entered the old, well-remembered gateway prison; not, however, as a buoyant visitor but as a papist prisoner in danger of forfeiting his life. He spent two months in the gateway's lightless insanitary dungeon, and nearly died from cold and hunger. Next, awaiting trial, he was escorted to the Fleet prison, London, where conditions were better. Due to the law's delay, and to the king's peremptory treatment of Parliament, Roe's appearance in the dock would be postponed for fourteen years. During that anxious time, apart from an occasional parole, he ministered to his fellow prisoners. The worst that could be held against him as he waited to stand trial for his life was that he enjoyed a drink and liked a game of cards.

War ended Roe's long wait. The Scots had taken up arms to defend, they said, their Protestant religion and their property rights: both causes were also equally dear to industrious English Puritans. The king, needing money to finance an English army, was compelled in May 1640 to summon Parliament, but the disgruntled Members, sympathising with the Scots, would not oblige. Charles responded by dissolving Parliament. Six months later, after the signing of a peace treaty with the Scots, and because of increased political tension, he had to re-call Parliament. It signalled the

3. *Alban Roe outside St Albans Abbey gateway in a stained glass window at the Church of Our Lady of Lourdes, Harpenden*

beginning of the end for Roe. Among other matters, Parliament was continuing to hound the royalist Catholics. A proclamation, reluctantly approved by Charles, banished priests; those remaining risked execution. Then, in January 1642, the day came when Roe stood in court at the Old Bailey to answer a charge of being an illegal priest. The judge, having insisted on a conviction, sentenced him to be hanged, drawn and quartered.

Twelve days later, on 31 January 1642, Roe and another similarly convicted priest, Thomas Reynolds, who was in his eighties, were tied onto a hurdle and dragged through the filthy streets from Newgate prison to Tyburn. The gallows at Tyburn was triangular, resting on three supports: hence 'Tyburn's triple tree'. It was a permanent structure with wooden galleries nearby which, on the occasion of an execution, were crowded. The old priest was terrified at the impending ordeal. Roe consoled him with words of comfort. 'I am,' Reynolds then assured Roe, 'in good heart, and I bless God for it; for I am glad to have as my comrade in death a man of your undaunted courage.' Gently, Roe helped him climb the ladder to the scaffold from where, cheerful as ever, Roe called to the crowd, 'Here's a jolly company!' He told them: 'I am guilty of no crime against the king or country.' He tipped the executioner with some beer money, telling him to serve God, do his job well, but not to get drunk. Mercifully, he and Reynolds were allowed to hang until dead before their bodies were cut down for the prescribed butchery.

The news of Roe's execution was proclaimed throughout the Catholic world in a mortuary bill published at Douai in February 1642. In stately Latin it announced that the Rev Fr Alban Roe had undergone martyrdom with a

*4. A plaque on a traffic island at the junction of Edgware Road and Bayswater Road, London, marks the site of Tyburn gallows.*

most courageous, eager and noble heart. As was usual in such circumstances, the announcement emphasised that his death was not owing to any treason: 'The grounds for his condemnation were his sincere profession of the Roman Catholic Apostolic faith, his priestly ministry, and his faithful exercise of that ministry for many years in bringing comfort to the Catholic people of the said realm.'

The mortuary bill ended on a note of hope: 'God willing, the life and death of this proclaimed martyr will become more widely known following this notice.' His life and death did not at once become more widely known in St Albans. However, by the end of 1642 a start had been made by the English Benedictines to obtain the honour of sainthood for their martyred brother. Political considerations and the exacting requirements of Vatican procedure combined to delay a decision until December 1929, when Roe was declared 'Blessed' — the first step to canonisation.

5. Alban Roe's mortuary bill, dated 8 February 1642, records his death.

During the intervening years among the first to relate his story in print was Richard Challoner. His *Memoirs of Missionary Priests*, published in 1741–42, relied for details of Roe's life upon original documents belonging to the English Benedictines at Douai. Thereafter, his memory was kept alive in various histories, notably Pollen's *Acts of the English Martyrs*, published in 1891, and Attwater's *Martyrs*, published earlier this century. More recently, in 1931, Roe was commemorated by Bede Camm in *Nine Martyr Monks*. About the same time, a stained-glass memorial window depicting Roe was dedicated at the Church of Our Lady of Lourdes, Harpenden. It shows him in the habit of a monk standing in front of the Abbey gateway. In his right hand he holds a knife, signifying the manner of his martyrdom; in his left, a book of the rules of the Order of St Benedict. The window heralded Roe's overdue return to the history of St Albans. Simultaneously, his canonisation was under consideration.

At last, on 25 October 1970, at a ceremony attended by Anglicans in St Peter's, Rome, the Catholic Church decreed that the name of Alban Roe, along with the names of thirty-nine other English and Welsh martyrs, should be inscribed in the catalogue of saints. Roe had spoken their epitaph: 'Here's a jolly company!' But by then, 25 October 1970, in St Albans, the place where he had discovered his vocation, St Alban Roe had long since joined the ranks of those in its hidden history.

Slowly, the mist of obscurity started to clear. Geoff Dunk, in one of his popular weekly articles on local history for the *St Albans Review*, told Roe's story in the issue of 24 September 1981. Local rehabilitation had begun. Eight years later, a souvenir booklet for a Benedictine week at the Cathedral and Abbey Church of St Albans included another account of Roe's life. And, on 21 January 1992, the three-hundred-and-fiftieth anniversary of Roe's martyrdom was commemorated ecumenically in the Abbey at a crowded Mass celebrated by Cardinal Basil Hume. Afterwards, the congregation was invited to pray in the old gateway for the unity of the Church. A lecture on Roe's life and work was given that evening in the Lady chapel by the Benedictine historian Dom Geoffrey Scott. Publicly, joyfully, St Alban Roe was being acknowledged in St Albans.

# 2
# GRIPING LANDLORDS DO TAKE ADVANTAGE

*The soil [of Hertfordshire] in general . . . but barren of itself without the great toil and charge of the husbandman.*
                                William Camden: *Britannia*


HERTFORDSHIRE sided with Parliament during the Civil War. But the county was not dumbly partisan. Five thousand of its inhabitants, among them people living in and around St Albans, seized a chance in 1647 to demand the righting of what they believed was an age-old wrong. Who were those people? What had provoked them into action?

A month before the war broke out in August 1642, a loyal attempt by the mayor of St Albans, William Neve, to proclaim support for Charles I, had ended ignominiously with Neve's jailing. The town's opposition to the king, like that of the other rebellious towns and counties, stemmed from years of royal interference in the making and keeping of hard-earned money. There had been forced loans in aid of the impecunious Crown: more than a hundred-and-sixty Hertfordshire gentlemen were compelled to appear before the courts to pay the various sums allotted. For small yeoman farmers, freeholders and copyholders — those entitled to hold land — there was a tightening noose of enclosure. Rents were rising. Prices, gradually but continually, were increasing. And there were tithes.

The payment of tithes, whereby lay people were required to contribute a tenth of their income (money or its equivalent in kind) to support the clergy, maintain

# GRIPING LANDLORDS 11

*6. The Royal Mail issued four postage stamps in June 1992 to commemorate the outbreak of Civil War in 1642. The stamps show soldiers from the opposing armies.*

churches and assist the poor, had been a long resented custom. Now, in a vastly changed post-Reformation England, the obligatory payment of tithes rankled still, especially among Dissenters separated from the established Church of England, which alone continued to enjoy the benefit of tithes. Some Dissenters, rather than pay tithes while denied freedom of worship, preferred to risk the tomahawk dangers of Massachusetts. Sixty-six of them, men, women and children, had gathered in St Albans in 1635 before setting out for the remote wilderness of New England.

Among those who stayed behind and supported the Parliamentarian cause, many believed, and were encouraged to believe, that the start of the war heralded the righting of every wrong. They had yet to learn that there sometimes are discrepancies between stated and unstated war aims. After all, both Charles and Oliver Cromwell vehemently maintained that each was fighting for liberty. Liberty involved religion. And 'Religion,' Englishmen were told by the poet John Dryden, who had begun publishing during the conflict, 'wheedled you to Civil War.' Of course, the wheedling did not lack venerable antecedents. There had been a century of national and international conflict in the name of religion. In 1642, as well as the religious divisions, there were fears among Parliamentarians that their ownership of former Church land might be endangered if the king should win the war. When he lost, those fears vanished in a scramble to acquire land vindictively confiscated from the Church of England. But Parliament continued to insist on the payment of tithes in an attempt to conciliate the clergy and secure its financial dependency. Property, religion and liberty were mighty links in a single chain.

Charles, having raised his standard at Nottingham, led his army south towards London in October 1642. From the capital, a Parliamentarian army marched through St Albans to intercept the enemy. The slowly-moving column of men and horses trudged up the steep slope of Holywell Hill, turned left, and plodded out of the town to fight the indecisive Battle of Edgehill, in Warwickshire, on 23 October. Thereafter, Hertfordshire, with a population of around thirty-six thousand, would be crossed and re-crossed by the armed forces of Parliament. The soldiers were not saints. More often than not their pay was in arrears, they were

7. *Robert Morden's map of Hertfordshire, 1704*

hungry and so they snatched the cluck or bleat of opportunity. Worse was to occur. Quotas of men were forced to join the rival armies; meanwhile, free quarters for them and their horses had to be provided in private houses.

Soldiers and civilians alike protested; there were dangerous social challenges, too, resulting in demonstrations and disturbances. A Hertfordshire petition to Parliament, presented in January 1643, sought protection for property owners 'from the violence and fury of all unruly and dissolute multitudes who endeavour to raise themselves by the ruin of your petitioners'. There were tumults. In May, 'disorderly, rude persons' at Shenley, near St Albans, removed the gates on common land enclosed by Edward Wingate, a Member of Parliament for the town and a brave captain in the Parliamentarian army. In July, excise, a new system of taxation, was imposed by Parliament on a range of goods, including ale, beer and cider. In December, three-hundred starving soldiers threatened to pillage St Albans on a market day but were dispersed. 'Liberty!' the loud, if confusing, battle-cry, was becoming louder.

8. *The Civil War made life harder for farmers.*

Accordingly, in February 1644, Hertfordshire householders petitioned against 'the intolerable burden of Free Quarters of many Horse and Foot'. In May 1646, two-thousand tenant farmers of Hertfordshire and Bedfordshire combined to present a petition against the payment of tithes. Their petition was rejected. Alarmed Members of the House of Commons told the petitioners 'that tenants who wanted to be quit of tithes would soon want to be quit of rent'.

A temporary lull in the fighting from midsummer 1646 to May 1648 failed to ease the social tensions. How could it? The failure of the harvest in 1646 — the first of six successive bad harvests — led to the price of bread being doubled. Maimed Parliamentarian soldiers were dismissed from the army to beg for a living. The unpaid remaining soldiers became mutinous: ten, at the end of 1647, were jailed in St Albans. People uprooted by the war wandered in search of work.

In May 1647, residents of St Stephen's parish, St Albans, were refusing to pay tithes or return expropriated church land to their recently appointed vicar. Yet another petition of grievances was submitted from Hertfordshire to Parliament in June 1647. In July, the town council of St Albans clamped down on the wanderers: 'No stranger, be he journey-man or servant, single or married, should remain in the Borough longer than six days without giving an account of himself to the Mayor. The officers of the Borough are directed to apprehend strangers and bring them before the Mayor to be sent back to the place of their abode.'

During the same year, the Hertfordshire tenant farmers again raised their voices in protest and, again, it was against the payment of tithes. This time, though,

9. *A Dutch woodcut, 1653, shows Oliver Cromwell seated in council.*

the persistent petitioners were the five thousand who had been provoked beyond endurance. Those farmers and others contended in their petition to Parliament that tithes encouraged the landlord to convert arable land to pasture, which brought him more rent for grazing than could the husbandman by ploughing it, and so the landlord neglected or pulled down houses, causing the depopulation of many villages. 'Tithes,' said the petition, 'have been the cause of the depopulation of many villages in the kingdom; for the landlord perceiving he can make more rent of his land to graze than the husbandman can give for it to plough, by reason that the tenth of his stock is taken from him; therefore, the landlord hath let fall or pulled down his houses and turned the land to pasture'. The petitioners argued that, 'The free gift of the people was the way that Our Saviour and His Apostles, and the ministers that succeeded them, had their maintenance,' and asked of the contemporary clergy, 'Are you ashamed to have your maintenance after this way?'

For good measure, the indignant farmers rapped other knuckles: 'Daily experience sheweth that many griping Landlords do take advantage . . . and have drawn their tenants to greater rents than they are able to pay.' The petitioners posed two more questions: 'Is there no year of jubilee for us, that our natural inheritance should return to us again? or are our ears bored that we and our children should be slaves to the impropriator and his children for ever?'

A tract of 1647, *The Husbandman's Plea against Tithes*, records the petitioners' persistence, and the names of some, but omits addresses. Nevertheless, among the names are those well known in and around St Albans. They include William Babbe, Thomas Berchmore, John Browne, Thomas Halsey, John Hare and John Humphrey; another signatory, William Rolfe, seems to be the only son of a yeoman farmer of St Stephen's parish. His surname was that which had been selected by the contemporary Catholic martyr Alban Roe when in need of an alias.

The anxious William Rolfe and the other wearied signatories of the petition were disappointed. Parliament did nothing about tithes. The execution of Charles in 1649, the ending of the Civil War in 1651 and the restoration of the monarchy in 1660 made no difference, either. Then and thereafter, until the beginning of reforms in the nineteenth century, the abolition of tithes could not only have threatened the existence of the Church of England but, more seriously, could have challenged fundamental rights of property: 'no tithes, no rent'. King and Parliament always had agreed: liberty never meant licence.

# 3
# WHO WOULD TRUE VALOUR SEE

*All people discontented; some that the King do not gratify them enough; and the others, Fanatiques of all sorts, that the King do take away their liberty of conscience.*

Samuel Pepys: *Diary, June 1662*

*10. St Peter's Church, St Albans, before its nineteenth century restoration*

THE unhappy distinction of being the only person to be shot in the Abbey Church of St Albans belongs to John Townsend. Little is known about him. Certainly, he was a member of a congregation of nonconformist Protestants at odds with the Church of England. Undoubtedly, his killing in 1662, two years after the restoration of Charles II, made it bloodily obvious to any who still might have thought otherwise that the Cromwellian days of limited tolerance for nonconformists were ended.

Some of Townsend's fellow citizens in St Albans are likely to have called him a 'Puritan'. The label was affixed widely and abusively to a Protestant nonconformist of any kind — Baptist, Presbyterian, Congregationalist, Quaker — and following the Restoration it implied, at best, disloyalty or, at worst, treachery. 'Puritans' were not to be trusted because they had been among the most active supporters of Parliament during the Civil War, using Bible texts to justify the overthrow of divinely ordained authority. And had not the Hertfordshire petitioners against tithes in 1647 dared to cite 'Our Saviour and His Disciples'?

'Fanaticks,' wrote John Dryden in the Preface to *A Layman's Religion* (1682), 'have detorted those Texts of Scripture, which are not necessary to Salvation, to the damnable use of Sedition, disturbance and destruction of Civil Government.'

Further outrages had been committed by 'Fanaticks' during the republican Commonwealth. Some of their ministers of religion were appointed to Church of England parishes. These ministers scorned vestments and ritual, and preferred their churches to be as unadorned as the pages of a ledger. After the Restoration, nonconformists like Townsend still practised where possible a form of worship that was plain and simple. But vestments make sacred authority visible. Ritual formalises worship. It reserves only for the ordained occupant of the pulpit the right to speak freely during a religious service. His voice in Restoration England was the voice of both Church and State. And in an age long before that of mass communications it often was the only voice. Religious conformity mattered: the kingdom that prayed together, stayed together.

*11. The passage through St Albans Abbey Church*

12. *Sir Harbottle Grimston*

'We shall be glad to think them true Englishmen,' Dryden continued, 'when they obey the King, and true Protestants when they conform to the Church Discipline.'

Nonconformity, however, did not exclude obedience to the king. Nonconformists of the Restoration period — Townsend included — were as ready as anyone to declare obedience. Their Protestant discipline required no conformity except that given freely to individual conscience. The radical dreams of the old, republican nonconformists were faded, and the location for the fulfilment of those millenary hopes had been removed irretrievably to the hereafter. Nevertheless, official suspicion of harmless nonconformists like Townsend persisted. The outcome was brutal intolerance.

Charles II had preceded his return from foreign exile with a declaration proclaiming a general pardon and liberty to 'tender consciences'. His new Parliament, however, wasted no time in restoring to the Church of England a position of unchallenged authority. Spiritual conformity and the sanctity of property went together, and laws were passed to safeguard both. The Corporation Act, 1661, limited membership of municipal councils to communicating members of the Church of England. The Act of Uniformity, 1662, required, among other things, ordination by a bishop for all ministers of religion. As a result, nationally, two thousand clergy were driven from their livings, fifty-seven of them from parishes in Hertfordshire, including the Rev William Haworth, the minister at St Peter's, St Albans.

The Act of Uniformity left little to chance: 'If any person above the age of sixteen shall be present at any meeting under colour of any exercise of religion in other manner than is allowed by the established Liturgy, where shall be five or more persons of the household, they shall for the first offence suffer three months' imprisonment, for the second offence six months' imprisonment, and for the third offence banishment to the American plantations for seven years; and in case they return, or make their escape, such persons are to be adjudged felons, and suffer death without benefit of clergy.'

The Conventicle Act, 1664, forbade the meeting of any religious bodies outside the Church of England, and the Five Mile Act, 1665, forbade nonconformist ministers to come within five miles of their parish or any town. Being a nonconformist, a 'Puritan', was risky.

The day of Townsend's martyrdom, Sunday, 4 May 1662, began on a sad note. Elizabeth, the wife of Charles Turrill, had died, and was to be buried in the cemetery at St Peter's. Fondly, the Rev William Haworth, who had been ejected to make room for a Restoration conformist, was invited by the congregation and the bereaved relatives to preach at the graveside. He was forbidden to do so by the new incumbent. Not to be thwarted, Haworth and the mourners decided to hold a memorial service at the Abbey Church. Only half-a-mile away, it had been bought by their ancestors as a parish church. Who would dare deny them access?

But rather than provoke a confrontation inside the Abbey, they assembled at the walled public passage which then cut through the building. The site of the shrine of St Alban was to the west; to the east was a schoolroom in the former Lady chapel. A hymn was sung, the Scriptures read, a prayer offered. By that time, the authorities had been alerted. They raised the

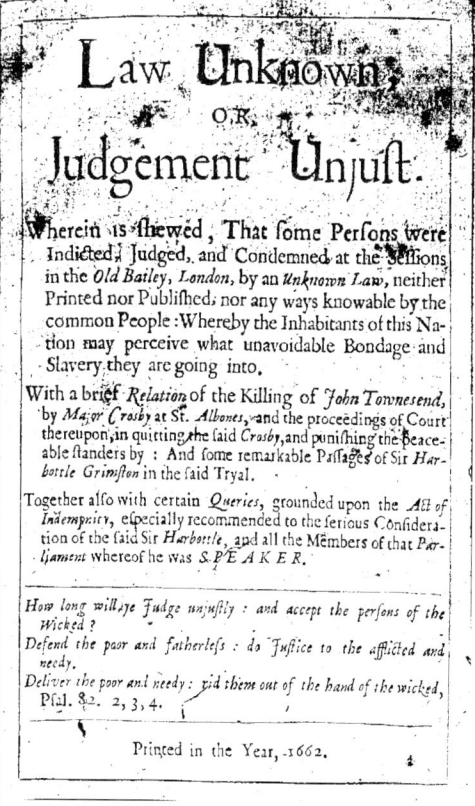

13. A tract published in 1662 denounced the trial proceedings following the death of John Townsend

alarm and, as Haworth stepped forward to give his memorial address, an angry officer of the militia, Major Edward Crosby, bustled forward. He called the mourners 'rogues', and, revealingly, 'rebels'.

'Why prate you there?' he shouted at Haworth. 'Come down, or I will pull you down.'

'If,' replied the minister, 'you have any authority to command me down, I will obey it, but otherwise, no.'

Outfaced, Crosby withdrew, threatening to bring reinforcements. He returned immediately, armed with a cocked pistol and accompanied by Timothy Ratcliffe, a parish constable, who held a fowling-piece. The frightened mourners gathered around Haworth. Crosby advanced. At that moment, Townsend stepped between the major and the minister.

'Noble major,' he said with serene politeness, 'pray make no disturbance; consider, it is the Sabbath day.'

'You rogue,' Crosby barked, 'do you tell me of the Sabbath day?' Furious, he lowered the muzzle of his upraised pistol, took aim, fired at point-blank range, and shot Townsend dead.

Legal proceedings were instituted. Haworth and those men in the congregation who had attempted to prevent violence were brought to trial at the Old Bailey in August 1662 on charges of instigating a riot. Crosby was indicted for murder. But between the foreman of the jury (none other than Timothy Ratcliffe) and the judge, Sir Harbottle Grimston (an eminent lawyer eager to gild the lily of his undoubted loyalty) justice would not be done, and would be seen not to have been done.

Grimston, as a moderate Puritan, had supported Parliament during the Civil War. Alarmed, however, by the Commonwealth radicals, he retired to private life, bought the Gorhambury estates on the outskirts of St Albans, and entered into secret negotiations for the restoration of Charles II. Chosen as Speaker of the House of Commons in April 1660, Grimston delivered an address of welcome to the king which is remembered as having been fulsome and servile in the extreme. Around the same time, he entered into an agreement with gamekeepers in St Albans to keep him supplied with partridge at the rate of sixty brace per annum. In November 1660 he was appointed Master of the Rolls of the Court of Chancery, for which rumour says he paid £8,000 in a bribe. On the other hand, according to Sir Henry Chauncy, a contemporary, he could be charming: 'He was a Person of free Access, sociable in Company, sincere to his Friend, hospitable in his Home, charitable to the Poor, and an excellent Master to his Servants.' Insofar as the trial was concerned, Grimston had conspicuous advantages. He knew St Albans: his eye would remain upon the defendants. He was their wealthiest local landowner. He was dependable.

Happily, something went wrong during the trial of Crosby. The jury, despite Ratcliffe being the foreman, found that the indictment of murder was correct: Crosby was guilty. Grimston was appalled: 'Will you hang a man upon supposition? Can you prove that he came with a full intent to kill Townsend?' He ordered the jury to reconsider, and brow-beaten, they rejected the indictment. Crosby was freed. The 'rioters' were bound over to keep the peace. Haworth was fined, and compelled to leave St Albans. He settled as a pastor of Congregationalists in Hertford.

An anonymous tract, published a week after the trial, exposed the travesty of justice. *Law Unknown, or Judgement Unjust* describes the killing of Townsend, relates the court proceedings and denounces Grimston for freeing Crosby and punishing the peaceable mourners. 'Some persons,' the tract states, 'were Indicted, Judged, and Condemned at the Sessions in the Old Bailey, London, by an Unknown Law, neither Printed nor Published; nor any ways knowable by the common People: Whereby the Inhabitants of this Nation may perceive what unavoidable Bondage and slavery they are going into.'

Townsend, the day after his killing, had been buried in the cemetery of the Abbey. His memorial, and that of similar martyrs, was raised by another and more famous nonconformist in the words of a challenging poem:

> Who would true valour see,
>   Let him come hither;
> One here will constant be,
>   Come wind, come weather:
> There's no discouragement
> Shall make him once relent
> His first avow'd intent
>         To be a Pilgrim . . .

John Bunyan included it in the second part of his allegorical masterpiece, *The Pilgrim's Progress* (1684). Bunyan, who lived in Bedford, is said to have preached and occasionally lodged in a cottage at Coleman Green, three miles north-east of St Albans. Nowadays, only a chimney of the cottage survives.

Nonconformity persisted in St Albans despite intimidation and persecution. Seven years after Townsend's martyrdom, a hundred Presbyterians were meeting every Sunday. Fifty Anabaptists managed without a regular place or time of meeting. Sixty Quakers met in a hired house every Sunday and Wednesday. A 'great number' of Congregationalists met in a private house. Is it probable that some were former members of Haworth's flock at St Peter's? If so, had they kept in touch with him since his removal to Hertford? And was their number increased greatly as a consequence of the manner in which Townsend died?

All the same, Townsend, who represented the conciliatory nature of Restoration nonconformity, had been a victim of chance although persecution motivated by redundant fears recurred. By the end of the century, however, both Church and State recognised the absurdity of hounding or, indeed, martyring individuals as unthreatening as Townsend. His fellow nonconformists were granted freedom of worship under the Toleration Act of 1689. They had reason to believe, perhaps, that Townsend's untimely death had helped.

*14. Rev William Haworth is commemorated in the vestibule of what is now the United Reformed Church, Hertford.*

# 4
# THE KIND PHYSICIAN

*Hope acts the kind physician's part,*
*And warms the solitary heart.*
                    Nathaniel Cotton: *Visions in Verse*


ST ALBANS provides the link in the lives of an exceptional physician and a renowned poet. Histories of St Albans have, however, tended to place Nathaniel Cotton (1705–88) in the shadow of William Cowper (1731–1800). But that is hardly surprising. Well remembered as the author of 'The Diverting History of John Gilpin', Cowper deservedly is more famous than Cotton who, as it happens, also was a poet. The link between them, though, was forged by Cotton's enlightened care of Cowper at St Albans during the stricken poet's first period of madness. The kind physician became his friend, gently bringing him back to a precarious sanity. It was gentleness that distinguished Cotton's methods in an age when the usual treatment of 'lunaticks' was harsh and punitive.

Cotton practised his healing art most notably at his private asylum for the mentally disturbed, the 'Collegium Insanorum'. Situated in what is now Lower Dagnall Street, and facing Spicer Street, it was an Elizabethan or early seventeenth century house which survived, in part, until finally demolished in 1910 to make way for a boot factory. College Street acknowledges by name that it occupies some of the site.

The son of a London merchant, Cotton studied medicine at Leyden. After obtaining his degree, he returned to England, assisted in a private asylum at Dunstable and, following the owner's death, opened his own asylum in St Albans in about 1735. Testifying, perhaps, to his gentleness his late employer's housekeeper and some of the patients moved with him. They occupied at least two successive houses in the vicinity of St Peter's Church before Cotton, as a result of increasing success, opened 'The College' in about 1760 with accommodation for up to ten patients.

Cowper was admitted in December 1763 and stayed until June 1765. After five months, and terrible agonies, he became milder. Cotton had treated him with great tenderness and skill. 'I was not only treated with kindness by him while I was ill,' Cowper recalled, 'and attended with the utmost diligence; but when my reason was restored to me, and I had so much need of a religious friend to converse with, to whom I could open my mind without reserve, I could hardly have found a fitter person for the purpose.' Believed to have accompanied Cotton to services at a nonconformist chapel in Lower Dagnall Street, he returned to St Albans for further treatment in 1768 and 1773. Another poet Cotton befriended was Edward Young (1683–1765), the rector of Welwyn, whose celebrated poem, *The Complaint, or Night Thoughts on Life, Death and Immortality*, became extremely popular both in England and Europe.

15. *Nathaniel Cotton*

Cotton, having settled in a house in St Peter's Street, which probably was the first in St Albans to be fitted with a lightning conductor, there directed the running of 'The College.' In 1738 he had married Ann Pembroke of St Albans, by whom he had eight children, but she died in 1749.

During the same year he published his only medical study, *Observations on a particular Kind of Scarlet Fever that lately prevailed in and about St Albans*. Scarlet fever, a highly infectious bacterial disease, killed many children or left them disabled with rheumatic fever, kidney disease or ear infections. Cotton's monograph, which demonstrates his abiding concern for the young, was the only

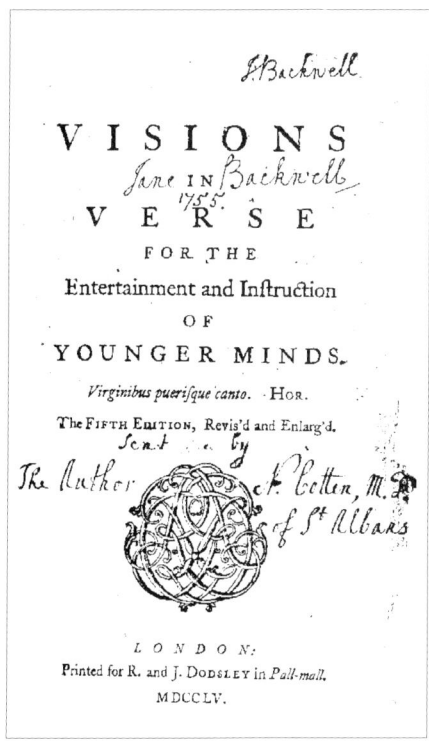

16. Title-page of Nathaniel Cotton's most popular work.

one of his works not to appear anonymously. In it he describes the then baffling disease's symptoms and his own treatment of an unfortunate four-year-old patient:

'He appeared quite bereaved of sense, almost suffocated, and at the point of death. Immediately I ordered him to be blooded to six ounces, speedily after which he revived, and came to himself. The child was naturally subject to enlarged Tonsils. But this symptom of strangling hastily came on, I think, within the space of half an hour, or thereabouts. On the fourth day, at two in the afternoon, it returned again with greater severity, if possible, than before . . . The Tonsils were swelled to that degree as threatened every minute to prevent all admission of air. Whereupon a Surgeon was called in, who attempted to relieve the child by making incisions in these glands. And so far the operation answered the end that the boy who appeared before in danger every moment of being suffocated, lived till about seven in the evening.'

At any rate, by the contemporary standards, the operation was a success even though the heroic boy died. Cotton, frankly and without elaboration, presented his conclusions:

'From the whole that I have advanced upon this disease, I think it appears that general rules of cure were precarious and uncertain; and that particular rules were not ascertainable on account of the various appearances and symptoms of the disease, and the various constitutions of various patients. And this perhaps furnishes a hint why mankind are so often disappointed in the perusal of medicinal writers. We are apt to expect too much from them; indeed, more than it is possible for the art to supply . . .

*17. Collegium Insanorum*

'So that it is in Medicine as in Navigation. Rules may be laid down and Charts exhibited; but when a man hath made himself master of all these, he will often find himself among shelves and quicksands; and must at last have recourse to his own natural sagacity to extricate himself out of these difficulties.'

Cotton's remarks reveal the man: modest, thoughtful, self-reliant, honest.

Two years after the *Observations*, in 1751, he married Hannah Everett of London, by whom he had three children. In the same year he published *Visions in Verse for the Entertainment and Instruction of Younger Minds*. According to the *Monthly Review* of February 1751, they were 'too grave', but they proved to be Cotton's most popular work and went into seven editions. They depict slander, pleasure, health, content, happiness, friendship, marriage and life and, in later editions, death. Cotton had written from the heart in a style calculated to appeal to literate and studious children. His intention was to proclaim the advantages of good health and true happiness because, as a physician, and devout Christian, he knew that the wages of sin were death. He knew, too, that syphilis caused insanity, and that rakes, no matter how dazzling, were likely to end their progresses as inmates of madhouses. *Visions in Verse* are the urgent words of advice of a kind and loving parent:

> Attend my visions, thoughtless youths,
> Ere long you'll think them weighty truths,
> Prudent it were to think so now
> Ere age has silvered o'er your brow:
> For he, who at his early years
> Has sown in vice, shall reap in tears.
> If folly has possessed his prime,
> Disease shall gather strength in time,
> Poison shall rage in every vein, —
> Nor penitence dilute the stain:
> And when each hour shall urge his fate,
> Thought, like the doctor, comes too late.

The work is not all admonition. Domestic scenes occur and it is tempting to suppose that Cotton, in the introduction, is describing his own home in St Peter's Street:

> I pass the silent rural Hour
> No slave to wealth, no tool to power.
> My mansion's warm and very neat;
> You'd say a pretty snug retreat.
> My rooms no costly paintings grace,
> The humbler print supplies their place.
> Behind the house my garden lies,
> And opens to the southern skies.
> The distant hills gay prospects yield,
> And plenty smiles in every field.

He gives high praise in the 'vision' of pleasure to the most famous son of St Albans, Francis Bacon (1561–1626), the philosopher and scientific pioneer:

> Are the dear youths to science prone?
> Tell how th' immortal Bacon shone!
> Who leaving meaner joys to kings
> Soared high on contemplation's wings;

> Ranged the fair fields of nature o'er
> Where never mortal trod before:
> Bacon! whose vast capacious plan
> Bespoke him angel, more than man!

Cotton admits the reader further into the secrets of his beliefs and opinions:

> You ask, What party I pursue?
> Perhaps you mean, 'Whose fool are you?'
> The names of party I detest,
> Badges of slavery at best!
> I've too much grace to play the knave,
> And too much pride to turn a slave.
> I love my country from my soul,
> And grieve when knaves or fools control.
> I'm pleased when vice and folly smart
> Or at the gibbet or the cart:
> Yet always pity where I can,
> Abhor the guilt, but mourn the man.

In the section on happiness, Cotton flings wide his compassionate arms:

> Come then, be mine in every part,
> Nor give me less than all your heart,
> When troubles discompose your breast
> I'll enter there a cheerful guest:
> My converse shall your cares beguile,
> The little world within shall smile;
> And then it scarce imports a jot
> Whether the great world frowns or not.

But it is a line in the section on pleasure which arrests and intrigues:

> And shall the soul be warped aside
> By passion, prejudice and pride?

Even as it stands, 'prejudice and pride' is a striking phrase, easily remembered and, for a child, easily reversed. And Visions in Verse consisted of the kind of elevated sentiments which the Rev George Austen, the cultivated rector of a Hampshire village, is likely to have approved. Did he provide his clever daughter, Jane, with a copy of Cotton's best-selling masterpiece? Cowper, coincidentally, was one of her father's favourite poets: 'My father reads Cowper to us in the evening, to which I listen when I can.' Did he read Cotton to her, too? And, long after, did the memorable words, transposed, return to Jane Austen in 1813 while casting about to retitle a novel she had revised?

Cotton's other successful poems, *The Fireside* and *To a Child of Five Years Old*, enjoyed a prolonged lease of life in anthologies, but nothing else of his verse found a large and lasting audience. After his death, his eldest surviving son, the Rev Nathaniel Cotton, rector of Thurnby, Northamptonshire, brought out a collected edition of his poetry, essays, allegorical stories, letters and sermons in two volumes.

Cotton, who died on 2 August 1788, is buried with his wives in the cemetery at St Peter's Church under an altar tombstone inscribed without dates or details: 'Here are deposited the remains of Anna, Hannah and Nathaniel Cotton.' Prosaic rather than poetic, it suggests characteristic contentment.

*18. William Cowper in the garden with his pets.*

# 5
# ABUNDANT CAUSE TO REMEMBER

*She stretcheth out her hand to the poor; yea, she reacheth forth her hands to the needy.*

Proverbs 31.2

VICTORIA Square, St Albans, is surrounded by unusually attractive office buildings. The area, which occupies the site of a Victorian prison, was redeveloped comprehensively in 1989, and part of the prison's high brick wall and imposing gateway were harmoniously retained. In the middle of the square is a large ornamental fountain. Nearby, a descriptive metal plaque is displayed. 'This fountain,' it states, 'designed by Sir Gilbert Scott was commissioned by a Mrs Worley in 1874 as a memorial to her son.' The staggering inaccuracies of the plaque compound its solecism: '*a*' Mrs Worley.

'Fame is,' indeed, 'like a river, that beareth up things light and swoln, and drowns things weighty and solid.'

When Mrs Worley died, on 30 January 1883, the city mourned. At Christ Church, in Verulam Road, the communion table, pulpit and reading desk were draped in black. During her funeral, a bell at the Cathedral and Abbey Church of St Albans was tolled. The curtains of private houses were drawn. Shops closed. Hundreds of residents lined the route of the cortège along London Road and Market Place to St Peter's Church. Hundreds followed on foot behind the hearse. Inside St Peter's, only relatives, immediate friends and invited mourners could be accommodated for the service; outside, at least two thousand people crowded the churchyard to pay their last respects to *the* Mrs Worley.

Mrs Isabella Charlotte Worley, born on 24 May 1817, was the youngest daughter of Joseph and Anne Timperon. There were three sons. They lived in the countryside, a mile or so south of St Albans, at Sopwell House, a large residence set in extensive grounds overlooking the River Ver. Early in the previous century it had been the residence of Edward Strong, the chief mason for Sir Christopher Wren in the building of St Paul's Cathedral. Strong's marble memorial is one of the splendours of St Peter's. In 1842, Isabella, and Henry Thomas Worley, a landowner and Justice of the Peace, of Dromenagh Lodge, Iver, Buckinghamshire, were married. They never had children. Four years later, Mrs Worley's father, who had made a fortune in the West Indies, died. Her brothers and sister also predeceased her, but it was with the death of her brother Arthur in 1855 that she inherited the fortune and the family home. During the same year, her mother died; so did her husband.

The three crushing blows failed to crush Mrs Worley. She was sustained by a profound, unshakable Christian faith, and it was as a practical expression of her

*19. Sopwell House, 1993*

faith that she committed her widowhood to the helping of those less fortunate than herself. She began by buying a church.

Seven years earlier, in 1848, Alexander Raphael, a newly-elected Member of Parliament for St Albans, and a wealthy Catholic, had offered to pay for the building of a church for his local co-religionists. They long had wanted their own place of worship: they accepted his offer. Raphael bought a defunct coaching inn and land in Verulam Road. Building work started immediately. The foundations were laid. The walls were rising when, unexpectedly, Raphael died in 1850. No provision had been made in his will for the church's completion, and construction ceased. The tiny Catholic community in St Albans, unable to shoulder the financial burden, withdrew from the project. Nothing more was done about the unfinished building until, in 1856, Mrs Worley intervened.

*20. Christ Church, St Albans, 1858*

The population of St Albans was more than six thousand, and increasing steadily. A railway to London via Watford was about to open; a direct rail link to the capital, when inevitably that arrived, would accelerate the expansion. Pews in a new church were unlikely to remain empty.

Mrs Worley bought the Verulam Road property, paid for its completion and, because she was an Anglican, presented it to the Church of England as Christ Church. The church's consecration was in April 1859. Catholics would have to wait nearly twenty years before obtaining a church of their own in St Albans. Meanwhile, Mrs Worley contributed most of the endowment, paid for the building of a vicarage and subsequently built the Christ Church school, which is now the local headquarters of the Royal British Legion. Altogether, her financial help in the Christ Church schemes amounted to not less than £11,000. She was getting into her stride.

Her next benefaction was to pay for the building of a nonconformist meeting place in Lattimore Road, St Albans. The plain single-storey timber hall, known as the Wooden Room, opened in December 1865; thereafter, Mrs Worley, attracted by the evangelical zeal of its congregation, became a life-long and generous member. Without rancour she had left the Church of England although she continued always to make annual donations to Christ Church. At the same time she financed the Wooden Room's gospel work, supported various orphanages and hospitals, including the St Albans Hospital and Dispensary, on Holywell Hill, and never failed to remember the poor.

It was with poor people in mind, especially wayfarers on their way to and from London, that in 1872 she offered to St Albans Town Council the gift of the ornamental drinking fountain. 'I wish it to be of benefit to the poor people,' she wrote to the mayor, Edward Wiles, during extraordinary negotiations over the siting of the fountain.

Designed by an eminent architect, the then Gilbert Scott, later Sir Gilbert, the nine-feet high fountain with three steps (not four, as in Victoria Square) consists of a bowl of polished Mull granite, weighing about three tons. In the centre is a crocketed finial of yellow Mansfield Wodehouse stone upon a deep moulding of Devonshire marble. Clustered columns of polished Peterhead granite support the bowl. Around the outer edge of the bowl is inscribed a text — doubtlessly selected by Mrs Worley — from St John: 'Whosoever drinketh of this water shall thirst again; but whosoever drinketh of the water that I shall give him shall be in him a well of water springing up into everlasting life.' Four bronze animal heads feed the water into the bowl and, originally, an overflow supplied a trough for dogs. Children were provided with an additional step on the opposite side. The fountain was made by a firm of sculptors, Farmer and Brindley, of Lambeth, and cost £500.

From the start the siting of the fountain caused a controversy which at times verged on the farcical. Gilbert Scott had proposed that the fountain should be placed at the High Street end of Market Place but clear of the Clock Tower. The town council preferred it on the French Row side in front of the Clock Tower. Traders objected to the council's preference. 'Besides being injurious to the houses of business,' said John Henry Buckingham in a letter to the *Herts Advertiser* on 6 April 1872, there would be the nuisance of 'children attracted to the spot to play with the aqua pura beverage, and the groups of idle, lounging, unrefined specimens of low life that will resort to it, contrasting comically with this beautiful specimen of art which the steps surrounding it are so well adapted for their indulgence.'

Buckingham, a talented artist, earned his living at a shop in High Street by selling antiques and paintings as well as by framing drawings and needlework, but is best remembered for his own crisp watercolours and fierce cartoons about local life. In 1868, one of his cartoons, depicting with glee the last agonies of a teetotaller, had made fun of Mrs Worley, although not by name, because of her support for what Buckingham called 'the Holy Cause of Teetwaddlism'. His letter to the *Herts Advertiser* continued by crediting Gilbert Scott with positioning the fountain so as to give plenty of room for any vehicle to drive around it, 'not to hide two sides of the fountain', as the council proposed, but placing it 'more conspicuously as an ornamental specimen of art, and commemorative of the benevolent object of the liberal donor'. Buckingham, perhaps, was offering an olive branch.

Most of the ratepayers in the Clock Tower's vicinity — a total of sixty — signed a petition protesting against the council's choice of site. Twenty of the tradesmen, who formed a deputation to the council along with many other objectors, were admitted to the council chamber when the location was discussed at a special meeting on 12 April. The deputation asked the councillors to reconsider siting the fountain in the centre of the square facing the Clock Tower, 'where it would be more ornamental and less objectionable than on the site which had been selected immediately in front of the tower'. A member of the deputation pointed out 'that by placing the fountain in the centre of the square it would not only be more ornamental, but it would form a protection to pedestrians crossing the street, many persons, especially elderly ladies, having been considerably alarmed in crossing that wide thoroughfare while vehicles were rapidly approaching'.

After further observations from the deputation, the council voted to discuss the question in private. Two hours passed before the council members, taking all things into consideration, reached a decision: that the 'most suitable' place for the fountain was in St Peter's Street in front of the Town Hall. The town clerk was directed to communicate with Mrs Worley, asking her approval of the site proposed.

Mrs Worley objected in a politely icy letter to the mayor: 'On giving the matter of the drinking fountain more attention, I think I should prefer it to be placed nearer the Clock Tower in the High Street, as I consider it would be almost useless in St Peter's Street, and would quite defeat the purpose I have in view, as I wish it to be of benefit to the poor people.' She had received 'a letter signed by several townspeople, who quite concur with me in this matter'.

The council, too, had received a letter. Signed by a hundred and thirty-eight ratepayers, it deprecated the idea of erecting the fountain in front of the Town Hall, and recommended the site facing the Clock Tower. There was no lack of advice. Another letter to the council, from a resident in High Street, suggested that the best site would be at the junction of George Street and Verulam Road. The council met to try again. Eighty of the townsfolk attended the meeting. Like the majority of their fellow citizens, they wanted the fountain to be in Market Place. The hapless councillors deliberated. The citizens present were impatient. They commented loudly. They hissed. At last, the councillors voted their approval for a site in Market Place — close to the spot first chosen by Gilbert Scott.

Spectators crowded the streets for the fountain's ceremonial unveiling on 10 June 1872. Flags fluttered on shop fronts, the Abbey bells pealed, but Mrs Worley was conspicuous by her absence. Pointedly, a speaker told the large gathering that her good works were done in the most quiet and charming way possible. The speaker continued, 'She has carried out that grand, Gospel principle that the left hand should not know what the right hand doeth.' Was he thinking of the town council? The delighted crowd cheered, and cheered again when the fountain was declared open. The mayor and other members of the corporation 'each drank a draught of the water, and the ceremony was brought to a close with three lusty cheers' for Mrs Worley. 'There was then a general rush of the crowd towards the

*21. The Wooden Room, St Albans, 1993*

fountain, and for some time afterwards the water disappeared as fast as the cups could be filled from the four flowing streams.' In the same report, the *Herts Advertiser* tempted fate by forecasting the fountain's future: 'No one will now say it is inconveniently situated.'

Mrs Worley continued her good works for the remainder of her life. Every winter she gave clothing and meat to the poor of St Albans. More than five hundred received clothes during the winter of her death. Many hundreds obtained gifts of meat at Christmas. One of her last kindnesses was to provide the children at Old London Road infants' school with buns and cakes for their Christmas treat.

'There are many besides ourselves,' said the Rev Henry Smith, the vicar of Christ Church, on the Sunday morning after Mrs Worley's death, 'who have abundant cause to remember the deceased with gratitude.' He reminded the congregation that her concern for the welfare of others was characteristic 'to the end'. And the widespread extent of the gratitude was demonstrated by the public reaction to her death: the silent, crowded streets, the respect. Worley Road was named in her honour. She was accorded by the *Herts Advertiser* the rare distinction of an obituary as its leader column: 'It is not all who, blessed with more than an ordinary share of the world's means, find it to consort with their particular feelings to display any large amount of benevolence to those needing assistance, but it seemed pre-eminently the characteristic of the late Mrs Worley to do the utmost which lay in her power to benefit in a variety of ways those wanting help... The poor of St Albans will miss a valuable friend.'

Contemporary directories had not ignored the town's poor. Readers were reminded that the churches in St Albans ran

*22. Mrs Worley's fountain in Victoria Square, St Albans, 1993*

clothing, coal, shoe and blanket clubs to which small weekly instalments were paid in order to obtain those necessities. A civic soup kitchen operated two days a week during the winter months. 'This institution,' commented the *St Albans Almanack* of 1882, 'has been, and it is hoped will continue to be, of great benefit to the deserving poor of the city during the inclement winter weather.' *Steven's Almanac and Directory* of 1883 reported that the soup kitchen had distributed 14,320 quarts of excellent soup to the necessitous poor of the town during its previous season. Mrs Worley would be missed.

A cousin, who lived elsewhere, inherited her fortune. Each of her domestic servants, and coachman, gardener, bailiff and stableman, received a year's wages; others received annuities. Sopwell House became an hotel. Verulam Golf Club took over most of the grounds. Christ Church was sold, in 1974, for commercial use; the Wooden Room awaited a similar transformation in 1992. As for the fountain, nine months only after Mrs Worley's death, the town council voted to re-position it on the spot selected by Gilbert Scott. Councillor William Hurlock, who had a whimsical sense of humour, suggested that the fountain should be put on wheels so that it could be moved from place to place when the members of the council changed their minds. But the fountain survived intact until the brutalities of the age of motor transport compelled its dismantling for street widening during the 1920s. By 1931, H.M. Alderman, in *A Pilgrimage in Hertfordshire*, was writing without regret of the 'miserable' fountain. The fountain itself disappeared, although the bowl was returned briefly to the site and filled with earth as a container for flowers. Its restoration, and re-assembly in Victoria Square, salvages a monumental portion of the city's past, and commemorates *the* Mrs Worley.

Her tombstone in St Peter's cemetery, and that of other members of her family, was removed prior to the building of a parish hall in 1982. 'Before the building began an archaeological dig was undertaken,' says *The Church and Parish of St Peter* guide-book of 1982. ' The foundations of the original North Transept (demolished in 1803) were confirmed but apart from a few miscellaneous bones nothing was found.' Diligently, members of St Albans and Hertfordshire Architectural and Archaeological Society charted the location of the tombstones before removal and recorded the inscriptions. The wording in relation to one of the deceased was in keeping with her life-long reticence: 'Isabella Charlotte Worley, daughter of Joseph Timperon, who died January 30, 1883, aged 65 years.'

# 6
# SIGN OF THE TIMES

*Hertfordshire public-houses . . . and their names are inseparably linked up in our past history.*

W. Percival Westell: *Historic Hertfordshire*

THREE closely intertwined strands connect a public house in St Albans to events of civic, national and international importance. No other public house in the city possesses a similar historical distinction; no other in Hertfordshire shares the name. *The Garibaldi*, at 61 Albert Street, while unambiguously honouring the nineteenth century unifier of modern Italy, also signifies contemporary agitation for social and political reform.

*The Garibaldi* opened in the mid-1860s as a beer-house for working men. Beer-houses, unlike hotels and public houses, sold beer or ale only and did not provide residential accommodation. At the time, St Albans, which then had a population of about seven thousand, was beginning to expand. Since 1858 a railway line had linked the town via Watford to London. Change was in the air. Changes for the better were expected. But St Albans lacked a voice of its own in Parliament. It had lost separate Parliamentary representation in 1852 as a result of notorious electoral corruption. All six hundred voters, including the middle-class householders entitled to vote under the long-awaited Reform Bill of 1832, were lumped in with those of a county constituency for Parliamentary elections. Their pressure to elect a St Albans Member of Parliament coincided with countrywide pressure for a second Reform Bill to extend the franchise to working men. And the return of the vote to St Albans could, for many of its citizens, mean a vote in the town for the first time.

Giuseppe Garibaldi personified the movement for social and political reform. In Great Britain and elsewhere working people saw him as one of themselves; in fact, he described himself as a working man. The son of a poor sea captain, he owed, in part, his enormous popularity to that ordinary background as well as to his outspoken radicalism. Freethinking, anti-clerical, he championed the rights of labour and women's emancipation, believed in racial equality and opposed capital punishment. He was admired, too, as a man of heroic action. Participation in a failed uprising against foreign oppression forced him when twenty-nine years old, in 1836, to leave Italy for South America. There, as a guerilla leader in wars of national independence, he first wore a red shirt. It became his universally famous emblem. The colour had no political significance: it was that of the cheapest cloth available to him and his penniless comrades. His return to Italy, in 1848, was followed by a dozen years of intermittent warfare, which culminated in the achievement of Italian unity in 1860. The British government had favoured the cause because unification made Italy an ally against France. Garibaldi, therefore, was admired, although for very different reasons, at every level of British society.

In St Albans the admiration was acknowledged and encouraged. Public meetings about him were expected to attract large audiences. But the number of people was disappointing at *Garibaldi and the Italian Revolution*, an illustrated lecture in the Corn Exchange, Market Place, during April 1861. 'The attendance was good,' the *St Albans Times and Herts Advertiser* reported 'although not so numerous as the subject deserved.' Another

23. *A general election advertisement in the Herts Advertiser of 21 November 1885 groups Lattimore with Cobden and Bright.*

lecture, however, on *Italy and the Great Garibaldi*, attracted a large audience to the Iron Room, Verulam Road, in February 1863, despite the 'deplorable state of the weather'.

The 'great' Garibaldi was the hero of several West End plays. His portrait graced the walls of mansion and cottage alike. A head and shoulders portrait painting on glass by an unknown artist had pride of place at *The Garibaldi*. And he received the ultimate Victorian acknowledgment of fame — depiction in various Staffordshire pottery figures. One of them, dating from about the time of his tumultuous visit to England in April 1864 shows the red-shirted hero holding a banner inscribed 'Liberty'. His arrival at Southampton filled two columns of the broadsheet *St Alban's Times and Herts Advertiser*. Subsequent coverage was equally extensive.

A Garibaldi mania had gripped the country. There were Garibaldi hats for men, Garibaldi blouses for women and, later, Garibaldi biscuits. A boy might have been fitted out in a Garibaldi jacket. It was not to everyone's taste. Years later, as though revealing an indiscretion, R.S. Garnett wrote in the introduction to his translation of Garibaldi's *Memoirs* (1931) that he had known 'a man who did not like Garibaldi. Why? He told me that at school he had been forced to wear a "Garibaldi" — a garment which he detested.' All the same, it was a good name. And its resonance persisted into the next century. Writers as different as Kenneth Graham in *The Wind in the Willows* (1909) and H. G. Wells in *The History of Mr Polly* (1910) could invoke with confidence the great name. Nevertheless, it was a name with undertones of republicanism, revolution and reform. To proclaim it, as did the first owner of *The Garibaldi*, was to taunt.

The owner, a member of the numerous Lattimore brewing and farming family of Wheathampstead, had a pecuniary motive: the tax on malt. The tax, which produced £6m a year for the Exchequer, infuriated the brewers and barley-growers, of whom there were many in Hertfordshire. Consequently, when a county Anti-Malt Tax Committee was formed in 1864 its participants included Charles Higby Lattimore (1807–89), of Place Farm, Wheathampstead. Earlier, despite the hostility of his fellow farmers, he had campaigned vigorously against the protectionist Corn Laws, which kept the price of wheat high. It is his involvement in that campaign which indirectly links him with Garibaldi.

One of Lattimore's fellow campaigners in the Anti-Corn Law League was the Liverpool-born politician and businessman Sir Joshua Walmesley (1794–1871). He became a patron of the painter Charles Lucy (1814–73), who specialised in painting large pictures deriving from English history and who, as a young man, had begun his career by painting an allegorical work in celebration of the Reform Bill of 1832. Walmesley commissioned him to paint a series of portraits of eminent men, including Cromwell and Nelson and the anti-Corn Law leaders, Richard Cobden and John Bright, and Garibaldi. Bright had spoken at a public dinner given by Lattimore in St Albans in March 1845 to honour a farmer who had exposed the grievances of the Game Laws. 'I am delighted to see this meeting,' Bright said, 'because I take it to be a sign of the times, and a sign of better times . . . '

Following the repeal of the Corn Laws in 1846, Lattimore remained an active Liberal and social reformer, supporting Home Rule for Ireland, until he died. Lattimore Road, in St Albans, is named after him.

24. *'The old Garibaldi Tavern', by Holmes Winter, 1898.*

But it appears to have been another member of the family, Ann Eliza Lattimore (1816–79), of High Street, Wheathampstead, who owned *The Garibaldi*. Presumably, she as of right had named the beer-house. What, though, prompted her choice of name? There was, no doubt, the infuriating malt tax, and she was a brewer. Might she have also been influenced in her bold choice by Garibaldi's support for women's emancipation? In any case, a whiff of radicalism in the name of one of the family's beer-houses might, perhaps, help keep the minds of political supporters and opponents concentrated. Besides, there remained the prospect of electoral reform. Garibaldi's name was useful, too, in that regard. Agitation was widespread. Indeed, another St Albans beer-house for working men, in Hatfield Road, proclaimed itself as *The Reformer*. A wider franchise and, for St Albans, re-enfranchisement, held out the hope of a government more responsive to popular demands.

The malt tax was not abolished until 1880, but an intensified effort to win the extension of the franchise had resulted in the Second Reform Bill of 1867. Under the Bill, working men of the towns received the vote; agricultural workers were left voteless until 1884, after which, in 1885, St Albans at last was re-enfranchised as a separate, although grotesquely enlarged, constituency. *The Garibaldi*, thanks to the associations of its name, recalls the Second Reform Bill victory.

A year later, in 1868, *The Garibaldi's* landlord, Henry Hibbert, found himself challenged by the law. At that time it was illegal to open on Sundays before one p.m. and Hibbert was caught selling beer at nine-forty a.m. He pleaded guilty at the Borough Petty Sessions on 30 December 1868, and was fined two shillings and sixpence (about twelve pence) with ten shillings (fifty pence) costs. It was an occupational risk. Beer-house landlords, catering for thirsty men who worked early and late, were harried by the police; hoteliers, serving a wealthier clientele, were protected. Hibbert survived. He remained as landlord after the premises were bought in 1872 by John Lloyd, a wealthy brewer and maltster, of Verulam Road, St Albans. Benskin's, the Watford brewers, took over in 1889. Significantly, neither of the new owners risked, as often happened, changing the name.

Literary mention of *The Garibaldi* had been made in 1884. Thomas Martin, landlord of *The Harrow*, Verulam Road, and an active member of St Albans Licensed Victuallers' Association, wrote *The City Pubs*, an entertaining list in couplets, which includes:

There's old Garibaldi with a flaming-red coat,
The savage White Lion and the tame little Goat . . .

Remarkably, there was clerical mention. The Rev Canon Edward Liddell (1845–1914), an honorary member of the Loyal Alban Lodge of Oddfellows, drew the attention of lodge members to *The Garibaldi* in a lecture in January 1893 on the streets, sites and signs of St Albans. 'Some of the signs are historical,' he said, 'such as the Fleur de Lys, the Red Lion, the Garibaldi . . . '

He had a practical reason for giving the lecture: 'If what I have said has reminded us that we are citizens of no mean city, and that we are each of us, therefore, bound to maintain and raise to a higher level the tone of the city in which we are privileged to live, my time and yours will not have been wasted in thinking about the streets, sites and signs of St Albans.' Liddell knew from experience about raising the tone of a place. In St Albans he was collecting money to build a chapel at the Workhouse for the use of the inmates: it opened in December 1893. A decade and more earlier, in Jarrow-on-Tyne, his selfless efforts to improve the lives of the iron and chemical workers led to a breakdown in his own health. He had come to St Albans to recuperate.

25. Garibaldi's portrait was returned to The Garibaldi in 1991. Flanking Alice Brown, the donor, and Richard Fuller, a director of Fuller's Brewery, are the public house's manageress, Anna Quick and manager, Paul McFarlane.

By 1898, when the 'old Garibaldi Tavern' was depicted in a collection of topographical etchings, Liddell had moved to Welton, near Rugby. The etchings, *The Last of Old St Albans*, were published by Holmes Winter (1851–1935), a self-styled 'historical painter', who lived in Hill Street, St Albans.

Garibaldi's death in 1882 had been followed in 1885 by the death at fifty-two of Hibbert. His widow, Eliza, who was left with three daughters and a son, took over the running of *The Garibaldi* and an adjacent butcher's shop, which had been established by her husband. Conveniently, a licensed slaughter-house was located in the out-premises of *The Garibaldi*. Mrs Hibbert's chances to relax must have been few. When she did dare to sit down it was only in a wooden armchair, and she always sat upright. She died in 1933 at the age of ninety-three.

Long before then, when retiring at the turn of the century, she went to live in Lemsford Road, St Albans. Among the prized possessions she took with her was Garibaldi's portrait on glass. After her death the portrait passed to a great-granddaughter, Alice Brown, of Watson's Walk, St Albans, and there it ended up in a cupboard under the stairs. In 1991, Miss Brown presented the portrait to *The Garibaldi*, where it was again put on public display. 'I thought I would like it to come home,' she told the *St Albans and Harpenden Observer*.

The portrait nearly had no old home. Over the years, as its trade expanded, *The Garibaldi* had been enlarged in piecemeal fashion. For instance, there was no internal communication between the public and private bars. 'The arrangement,' the Chief Constable, Nelson Ashton, told the St Albans Licensing Justices in 1932, 'is not desirable for the purpose of police supervision.' Concurring, the justices deferred renewing the licence. An anxious month ensued. Then, at a renewed hearing, Gerald Block, appearing for Benskin's, argued that *The Garibaldi* should be maintained to serve the needs of the district. 'It has a substantial trade of two-hundred and seventy barrels a year,' he said, according to the *Herts Advertiser*. The justices reconsidered, and decided to renew the licence, providing the Chief Constable's supervisory requirements were met. *The Garibaldi* was saved. It had already been selected by W. Percival Westell in *Historic Hertfordshire* (1931) as a public house with a notable name. And the name stayed when the premises were purchased by Fuller's in 1985.

'This well kept, refurbished Victorian place,' said The *1991 Good Pub Guide*, 'centres round the island servery, visible from the little tiled-floor snug up some steps; a separate food counter on a lower level opens out into a neat and cosy little no-smoking conservatory. It's often notably lively, not least when a fairly regular crowd of mainly youngish people gathers there.' The popularity of the venue is a reminder of the popularity of Giuseppe Garibaldi himself.

# 7
# KEPT BACK BY FRAUD

*Who is to dig it? Which of us, in brief words, is to do the hard and dirty work for the rest — and for what pay?*

John Ruskin: *Sesame and Lilies*

RURAL hopes were high in the summer of 1872. Throughout England, throughout Hertfordshire, the long-suffering farm worker was campaigning with renewed determination for an improvement in his conditions. Cruelly overworked and grossly underpaid, his life was that of a beast, except a beast was likely to occupy better accommodation. His average wage was no more than fourteen shillings a week in Hertfordshire. In London, unskilled labourers received eighteen shillings; gas factory stokers, thirty-eight shillings. And, every summer, the farm worker could be out in the fields from early dawn to late sunset.

Edwin Grey, recalling Harpenden during the 1860s–70s in his *Cottage Life*, says that farm hands, both boys and young men, had to rise at four o'clock. Ploughing finished at two o'clock, but the horses had then to be watered, cleaned, combed, the stable littered, and the animals fed and made comfortable. 'At harvest and hay times the hours were much longer — the men working sometimes until nine o'clock or past.'

Equally brutal were the farm worker's domestic conditions. Samuel Smiles, in *Thrift*, an 1875 sequel to his best-selling *Self-Help*, wrote: 'The agricultural labourers have not decent houses, — only miserable huts, to live in. They have but few provisions for cleanliness or decency. Two rooms for sleeping and living in, are all that the largest family can afford. Sometimes they have only one. The day-room, in addition to the family, contains the cooking utensils, the washing apparatus, agricultural implements, and dirty clothes. In the sleeping apartment, the parents and their children, boys and girls, are indiscriminately mixed, and frequently a lodger sleeps in the same and only room, which has generally no window, — the openings in the half-thatched roof admitting light and exposing the family to every vicissitude of the weather.'

Very few cottages enjoyed adequate sanitation or, from the customary well, clean drinking water. Sandridge, for instance, in 1872, was in a lamentable condition regarding its drainage and provision of water. 'Cottages,' the *Herts Advertiser* editorialised in January 1872, 'are entirely without sewage receptacles, and as a natural consequence certain of the inhabitants, not very scrupulous in cultivating habits of cleanliness and common decency, actually throw their sewage and refuse into the highway.'

26. *A farm worker wearing 'that ancient and picturesque garment', a smock.*

Of course, cleanliness is an easy option at the turn of a town tap while simply to exist in a slum, exhausted by monotonous toil, poverty and hunger, induces apathy. The wonder is that the farm worker roused himself at all to secure better conditions. And yet, a generation earlier, in 1839, men from Hertfordshire villages, such as Hatfield, attended radical meetings on Parliamentary reform in Greensted, Essex. The organiser was George Loveless, one of the transported trade unionist Tolpuddle Martyrs, newly returned from Australia. During the

1860s, the Hertfordshire men formed a short-lived trade union. In 1867, they supported a strike by farm labourers in neighbouring Buckinghamshire. By early 1872, their stubborn hopes were rising again. In February, Joseph Arch, a Warwickshire agricultural labourer and Primitive Methodist lay preacher, had responded helpfully to appeals from fellow farm workers to form a trade union for them.

Arch already was committed to a year of action but of a different though not dissimilar kind. Along with his co-religionists he was preparing to mark the centenary of the birth of one of the denomination's founders with an intensive programme of spiritual events. Might not the founder's commemoration and the union's formation fruitfully coincide? Was not practical Christianity their common ground? Besides, Primitive Methodists were distinguished by their prowess in preaching at open-air meetings. For Arch, and others like him, it was a talent that would be put to wider use. The outcome, at the end of May, was the National Agricultural Labourers' Union — the farm workers' first national trade union. Its main aims were a weekly wage of sixteen shillings and a nine-and-a-half-hour working day. As usual, the farm workers' aims were modest: engineering workers already had won a nine-hour day. Farm workers thronged to the new organisation. They included those who joined at a meeting held during a cloudy June evening on Nomansland Common, three miles from St Albans, between Sandridge and Wheathampstead.

27. *Joseph Arch*

The meeting place, which had the considerable advantages of costing nothing and being spacious, was known widely as a location for sporting events. Gathered there that Thursday under the shelter of two great elms, and after a long day's work and, for many, a long walk, were five hundred farm workers with their wives and children. Leaflets headed 'Unity is Strength' had invited them to attend in support of the union's claim for 'a fair day's pay for a fair day's work'. The principal speakers came from a branch of the union established at Luton the previous week. William Paul (1821–1901) was elected the evening's chairman. Paul, of Sandridge, a respected carpenter with sufficient financial independence to risk the enmity of the farmers, took the farm workers' cause to heart. He told them that the union's representatives, knowing the tyranny and sort of serfdom under which they were labouring, would show them lawful and just means of releasing themselves from their present position. First, though, he would ask them to unite to become 'the most gigantic class of people in the country'. A resolution he moved was carried amid deafening cheers: 'It is the opinion of this meeting that it is necessary for the labourers to be united for their own protection.'

Evidence of their desperate need (and of a reporter's lofty condescension) appeared in the *Herts Advertiser* account of the meeting: 'Joseph Allen, a labourer who displayed intelligence above the average of his class, said that until lately he had only been receiving eleven shillings a week, but he now had twelve shillings. Of this amount he had to expend four shillings a week in rent, firing and candles, which left him eight shillings for the maintenance of himself and family. He had had six children, but he had lost three (a voice: "A wonder you haven't lost 'em all"). He reckoned that his wages allowed twopence-halfpenny a day for each member of his family to live upon ("shame"), and how any man could live upon that he did not know. Many had been obliged to work hard all day, and sometimes had nothing but a piece of bread, and sometimes a red herring (laughter and a voice: "That's about right, Joe"). They found it was written in the Scriptures "Blessed is the man that considereth the poor; but cursed is he who grindeth the face of the poor." Then again in the fifth chapter of St James's Epistle it was said "Behold, the hire of the labourers who have reaped down your fields, which is of you kept back by fraud, crieth: and the cries of them which have reaped are entered into the ears of the Lord of sabaoth." They might rest assured that the Lord knew all about it (hear, hear). They found it very hard and a very solemn thing to keep themselves from one week to another, and they scarcely knew how to do it. In harvest time, however, they managed to earn a few shillings extra, and then they managed to buy the children some clothing as well as they could (a voice: "And what you can't pay for goes unpaid").'

Conspicuous among the shabbily-dressed crowd was the Rev Canon Owen William Davys, Rector of Wheathampstead. Son of a Bishop of Peterborough, and with fourteen servants to look after himself and his family, he tended to find the farm labourers quaint. Indeed, he recalls in his autobiography, *A Long Life's*

*Journey*, (1913) that when preaching his first sermon in Wheathampstead in 1859 — and he was preaching there till he died in 1914 — he did not expect to see farm workers wearing smocks 'but to my joy found some half-dozen elderly wearers of that ancient and picturesque garment sitting on forms beneath the pulpit'. Although bewildered by the farm workers' campaign, he sympathised, unlike Dr Ellicot, the Bishop of Gloucester, who suggested that agricultural union agitators should be thrown into the village horse-ponds. In a private list drawn up by John Edwin Cussans, the author of *History of Hertfordshire*, Davys occupied third place among the six men in the county whose handwriting was the most illegible. His hobby was collecting ferns. He also restored his parish church, St Helen's, Wheathampstead, built the village school and enjoyed archaeology.

Accepting an invitation to address the labourers, Davys assured them that he did not speak in the interest of the farmers: he often had to find fault with them. For example, very recently he had to complain of one who took thirty children out of the school to pick charlock. Actually, he would be only too thankful if he could see his way clear to every labourer being paid £1 a week; at present, he could not.

A pound a week signified paradise regained. Flora Thompson, recalling country life of the 1880s in *Lark Rise to Candleford* declares, 'Queenie's ideal of happiness was to have a pound a week coming in. "If I had a pound a week," she would say, "I 'udn't care if it rained hatchets and hammers."

Still, Davys did see his way to a steady, gradual rise in wages, if only the labourers had patience. And the kindly labourers did not lose their patience openly until Davys ascribed nine-tenths of the misery and wretchedness and poverty of

28. *Canon Owen Davis.*

the labouring classes to the fact that they did not take sufficient care of their money. His tactless remark provoked shouts. Other things said at the meeting, and not reported, appalled the *Herts Advertiser*: 'One or two of the speakers were unsparing in the uncomplimentary epithets and the scurrility — we had almost said blasphemy — they directed against the upper classes and the farmers . . .'

Miraculously, no avenging thunderbolt had struck. It was a Wheathampstead resident more widely known than the rector who rained the fire and brimstone of his anger upon the farm labourers. Charles Higby Lattimore, veteran campaigner for the repeal of the Corn Laws and critic of the power of landlords over tenant farmers like himself, adamantly opposed the farm workers.

29. A collector's indoor fern pillar.

He urged other farmers to take united action against the union members, advocating the imposition of lock-outs and the keeping of blacklists. Did it worry the ferocious old radical that *The Garibaldi* public house in St Albans, owned by a member of his family, commemorated a champion of the rights of labour?

The union persevered. Encouraged by support received, it kept up the pressure. Another meeting was held the following week — on Harpenden Common — when as many as eight hundred people were estimated to have been present. 'Many of them,' the *Herts Advertiser* of 15 June reported, 'were persons who had evidently come to gratify the curiosity very naturally excited by the novelty of the meeting, and not from motives of personal interest in the matter.' Be that as it may, the newspaper was glad to notice 'the absence of a certain discreditable kind of stump oratory . . . and that as a whole the speeches were more temperate and rational in their tone'.

In his temperate and rational speech, William Butler, of Harpenden, said that the wages were too low, and consequently the men and their families were badly clothed and badly fed. 'Every farmer knew perfectly well that his men were badly paid (hear, hear, and a voice: "That they do"), and no arguments were needed to enforce the fact.' All the same, he firmly believed that the masters would eventually give the increase. There was tremendous cheering when a resolution supporting the union was put to the meeting and carried.

An anonymous writer of the time put the farm workers' hopes into the words of a song, *The Roast Beef of Old England*. It ends:

> So stand by the Union, the winter's gone through,
> Neither hunger nor cold could our courage subdue,
> For there's one thing we want, and mean having it too:
> > The jolly roast beef of Old England,
> > The glorious Old England roast beef.

The farm workers' hopes remained high and their new inexperienced union flourished as its organisation ripened with the summer. More meetings were held. Two, at Colney Heath and Bernard's Heath, on the outskirts of St Albans, were rowdy. 'For a time,' at the second meeting, according to the *Herts Advertiser* of 3 August, 'the labourers listened quietly enough to the invectives with which bishops, clergy, aristocracy, farmers, and indeed everybody holding any position in the social scale above that of an agricultural labourer, were anathematised; but when the speakers warmed to their subject, and conjured up before their hearers a host of imaginary evils, the enthusiasm of the latter knew no bounds, and they cheered, shouted, and yelled to an unlimited extent.'

Could it be that the farm workers, after years of tugging forelocks reluctantly, were learning to enjoy the freedom of cocking a conspicuous snook? They had been tempted sorely. Indeed, when a man in the crowd at Bernard's Heath disagreed with a speaker, he was knocked down and kicked. William Paul, the respected carpenter of Sandridge, intervened and saved the audacious man from being thrown into a nearby pond. The farm workers, in their own way, had been attempting to do no more than follow the advice of the Bishop of Gloucester.

In any case, the justice of their cause was undeniable. An editorial in the *Herts Advertiser* on 3 August made it plain: 'That the labourers can show a good case no one can doubt; that their wages must and ought to be increased is equally certain. How they and their families have managed to live on twelve or fourteen shillings per week has often excited our surprise; nor do we believe the employers, as a whole, are adverse to a fair and moderate rise.' Soon, agricultural wages rose by an average two shillings a week throughout the country.

The slightly better times did not last. After 1875 huge quantities of cheap wheat were imported from the United States, and British farming went into a depression from which it did not begin to recover until the outbreak of the First World War in 1914. The union, however, although its strength declined, had given the farm workers an awareness of their own economic power when united. In the forelock-tugging world of nineteenth century Hertfordshire it was an unforgettable lesson and fostered the farm workers' desire for political power. Increasingly, they demanded the vote. And in the organised expression of that desire, as in the formation of the first national agricultural labourers' trade union, St Albans participated.

On 3 March 1873 a large meeting of agricultural labourers was held in the Corn Exchange, St Albans, and a resolution was passed asking the House of Commons to extend the borough franchise to the counties of England. The campaign took another eleven years but when the Reform Bill of 1884 was passed it enfranchised the long-suffering fellows who followed the plough.

# 8
# THE BATTLE OF SANDPIT LANE

*Spoke out the nameless Leader,*
  *'That Railing must go down.'*
*Then firmer grasped the crowbar*
*Those hands so strong and brown.*
*They march against the railing,*
  *They lay the crowbars low,*
*And down and down for many a yard*
  *The costly railings go.*
      Anon: *A Lay of Modern England*

ACTIONS spoke undeniably louder than words in St Albans during the summer of 1884. Since early that year common land alongside Sandpit Lane had remained impertinently and illegally enclosed. Townsfolk objected without effect. Meetings of the city council echoed with indignant sound and fury, signifying nothing much, until the townsfolk themselves, their patience exhausted, and to preserve something familiar in their fast-changing town, took direct action.

A thousand of them, working hard, put paid to the enclosure of the common land on the south side of the lane from near Stonecross to the junction with Lemsford Road. Afterwards, their work successful, the jubilant crowd marched singing through the city before dispersing peaceably. To this day, the land they reclaimed remains public and open.

54   THE BATTLE OF SANDPIT LANE

There was a price to pay. Six of the demolition activists — William Giddens, Edwin Toms, Harry Wakefield, labourers; Edgar Crowhurst, a dealer; William Hilliard, an ex-lawyer's clerk; Thomas Martin, a one-legged pedlar — and two of the instigators, William Westell, a straw hat manufacturer, and William Hurlock, a draper — both were city councillors — stood trial before county magistrates in the court room of the Town Hall. Magisterial disdain was a feature of the two-day trial. Underlying the hostility between the chairman of the bench and the defendants were deep differences in outlook, especially concerning change.

Change mattered most. Its consequences had recently transformed the appearance of the ancient Cathedral and Abbey Church of St Albans as a result of controversial renovations designed by a wealthy Yorkshire barrister, Sir Edmund Beckett — later Lord Grimthorpe — who, coincidentally, was chairman of the bench at the Sandpit Lane trial. He was in no doubt that change, if ordered by himself, would always be for the better. But change was changing the whole of St Albans out of recognition.

'Of late years the city, and especially the north-eastern part of it lying between Bernard's Heath and the Midland [City] Railway Station has very much increased, and is still increasing,' wrote Frederick Mason in his *Illustrated Handbook* of 1884. He continued, 'A considerable portion of land, known as St Peter's Park, has been planted and laid out for the erection of villas, new roads have been made, and these will form a pleasant addition to the suburbs of the city. Other estates in the same quarter have been sold for building purposes.'

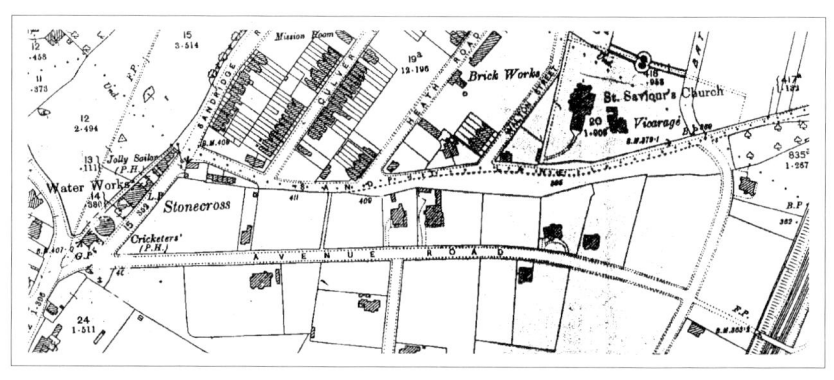

30. An Ordnance Survey map of 1898 shows the common land on the south side of Sandpit Lane.

Did it seem that all the old surroundings would disappear under a barrage of bricks and mortar? Indeed, a district had sprung up rapidly around the City Station after its opening for passenger traffic in 1868. There already were eleven thousand inhabitants in the town. Surely, some corner of the place could be kept undeveloped, unaltered?

As it happened, it was the change from open fields to the building sites of St Peter's Park that prompted the change from open space to enclosure. Sandpit Lane runs roughly parallel to Avenue Road where, from the back garden of a house belonging to John Wells, a jeweller, and that of his neighbour, Frederick Austen, a builder, the encroachment was mounted in February 1884. Wells' wire fence, stretching about four hundred feet alongside the lane, and Austen's short wooden fence incorporated the strip of common land which ranged in depth from five to eighty feet. Urban land, no matter how irregularly shaped, excites hopes of easy money for owners during a building boom. And John Wells, whose jewellery shop sparkled in Oxford Street, London, was a shrewd property speculator. Four years earlier, anticipating further expansion of St Albans, he had bought St Peter's Park. Only the awkward strip of common land separated his investment from Sandpit Lane. Why not consolidate the property? Why not enclose and enlarge? Austen agreed, and up went their fences.

31. William Hurlock

Protest was predictable. Councillor William Westell, the straw hat manufacturer of Holywell Hill, St Albans, objected to the enclosure at a city council meeting on 20 March 1884. It was, he said, a clear encroachment and it was perfectly open to anybody to pull the fences down. His friend and fellow Liberal, Councillor William Hurlock, also of Holywell Hill, thundered support: 'There is no doubt that the whole of this land in Sandpit Lane belongs to the public, and that it is a case of clear encroachment ... It is simply a system of robbery.' Cautiously, the council voted to obtain more information which, when the council next met, in April, was received in private.

Westell (1831–901) and Hurlock (1840–1925) were friends. Hurlock, first elected to the council in 1874, had taken part in the agitation of that year which, after the closure of the public passage through the Abbey, secured a right of way footpath around the east end of the building. During that agitation, and to enliven it, Hurlock hired a brass band who, asking what to play, were told, 'See, the Conquering Hero Comes.' The instruction, half-serious, half-humorous, was pure Hurlock. Less spectacular in manner, Westell, with Hurlock's public support, had been elected to the town council in 1880. In 1876 he had helped form Hertfordshire County Cricket Club. Together, the two men were formidable.

Meanwhile, a prominent agitator with a national audience had spoken out against enclosure. Joseph Chamberlain, a Liberal Member of Parliament for Birmingham and President of the Board of Trade, told the House of Commons on 27 March during the second reading of the Reform Bill that would enfranchise the agricultural labourer: 'You cannot go into a single country lane in which you won't find that the landowners on each side of the road have enclosed or are enclosing lands which for centuries belonged to the people.' It was not an entirely disinterested observation: 'Brummagem Joe' had an eye on the rural vote.

But encouraged, perhaps, by Chamberlain's words, Westell tried again and, supported by Hurlock, proposed that Austen should be written to 'on the subject of extending his fence'. The resolution was reinforced by another at a council meeting on 23 April, when it was decided that notice should be served on Wells and Austen to set back the fencing where it encroached on the public highway.

The reference to the public highway was clumsy, and provided the enclosers with a chance to obscure the point at issue — the legitimacy of their encroachment. Gratefully, the phrase was seized on by Wells' lawyer brother, William, of Market Place, St Albans, in his reply to the council's notice. Avoiding reference to the encroachment, William Wells devoted his letter to a discussion of the measurements from the centre of the road to the fences as though the width sanctioned the position of the fencing which, legally, it did not. More brazenly, 'should any alteration of the fence be found necessary', he reserved the right for his client to put the fence forward!

The audacity proved to be too much for the city council, meeting on 2 May, but only after an ominously long discussion was it decided that proceedings before the magistrates should be taken against Wells and Austen.

Three special meetings of the council followed. At each, cautious members raised the bogy of legal costs and conducted lengthy examinations of legal niceties. Insults were exchanged. Hurlock, for instance, never hesitated to jump in with both feet when one would have been more than sufficient. It goes without saying that the fences remained, newly accompanied by a notice threatening trespassers on the enclosed land with prosecution. Strangely, no proceedings were taken against Wells and Austen; instead, the council members at their meeting on 21 May voted for more enquiries to be made concerning the enclosed land. Haste was being made very slowly. On 4 June, Hurlock told the members that the mayor, as the chief magistrate, could legally give an order to the surveyor to at once pull down the fence. 'Public rights are being infringed,' he declared, 'and I call upon the council to do what is necessary.'

But Councillor Henry Smith advised caution. He pointed out that he was as desirous of doing what was for the benefit of the city as were Councillors Westell and Hurlock. Then, in a moment of acute perception, he threw down a challenge: 'If Westell and Hurlock are so sure, why do not they themselves pull down the fence? Let them not bark without they can bite.'

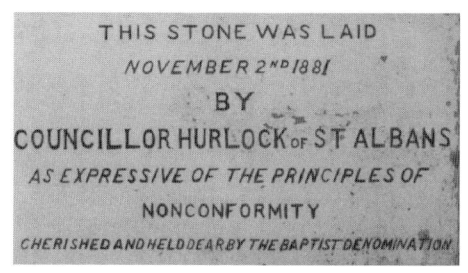

32. *Comrades in arms: memorial stones were laid at the Baptist Tabernacle, Victoria Street, St Albans, by William Hurlock and (33) Henry Taylor*

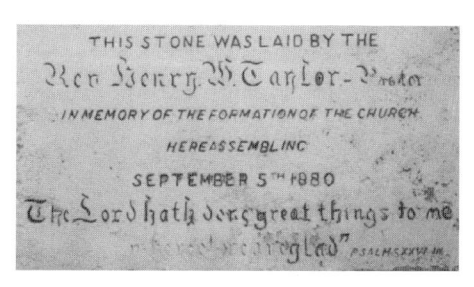

In fact, Westell and Hurlock, although regarding themselves as tribunes of the people, were businessmen primarily, not rebels: they wanted the biting to be done by the council and were opposed to private individuals taking action. True, they barked, especially Hurlock; they also voted in favour of a resolution, passed at the third of the special meetings, that counsel's advice should be taken in the matter of the encroachment. By then, 25 June, the disputed enclosure had lasted five months and it might have seemed that the law's delay, and the council's, would make it permanent.

Reinforcements were on the way. The Rev Henry Taylor, minister of St Albans Baptist Tabernacle,

Victoria Street, entered the fray by calling a public meeting in the Corn Exchange, Market Place, for Tuesday 15 July. It was crowded and it would be crucial. After all, the meeting concerned a place close to the heart of everyone in the room: St Albans. Pastor Taylor, a friend and co-religionist of Hurlock, was voted to the chair. A practised speaker, he wasted no breath: 'I wonder at the audacity of a man who can take such a piece of land from the public. I also marvel at the sweet sleep which the neighbourhood and the town council labour under in regard to the matter.'

Hurlock, who was present with Westell, is likely to have kept his face innocently expressionless.

More revelations — from the same impeccable source, no doubt — were related by Taylor. He had, he confided, had the 'opportunity of gleaning' counsel's opinion of the encroachment. The opinion had been known by the city councillors for at least two weeks, but a majority of them had voted to keep it secret 'as it would be unwise to show their hand to their opponents'.

*34. Sir Edmund Beckett (Lord Grimthorpe).*

The learned counsel, said Taylor, had pointed out that there was a beaten footpath by the side of Sandpit Lane, and that gave the public indefeasible possession.

Westell, after being invited to the platform, elaborated: counsel was of the opinion that the city council should require Wells to remove the fence, or failing that, take proceedings to compel its removal. Applause greeted Westell's contention that if the fence were pulled down that night, Wells could do nothing.

'Pull it down,' someone had shouted during Westell's remarks. 'Don't talk about it so much. Pull it down.' A young labourer at the back of the room agreed: 'Let us have it down.'

Hurlock's observations when he addressed the meeting were characteristic: 'The thieving propensities of the great land-owners are proverbial . . . Insist that the thousands of acres of land which have been stolen should be given back. . . . There are land grabbers throughout the country, and a few around St Albans . . .'

The temper of the meeting was militant — 'of an animated character', according to the *Herts Advertiser* — and a resolution expressing 'indignant protest against the wanton and illegal enclosure' was carried with only one vote against. Another resolution called for a deputation from the meeting to ask the town council to 'act with decision in the protection of the people's rights'. Headed by Taylor, the deputation and many supporters were received next day at the council meeting in the Town Hall. The room was packed. The exchanges were noisy.

Taylor, urging swift action, ended his appeal with a pertinent observation: 'The council are the guardians of the people's rights, and it is better that they should cause the fence to be removed constitutionally rather than leave it to a hurry scurrying crowd to do the work.' The warning was timely. A decision there and then by a majority of the councillors, settling once more for the taking of legal proceedings, upset the action-eager crowd. 'Pull it down,' some of them shouted. 'Pull it down.'

That afternoon, Wednesday 16 July, fifty or so hurry scurrying labourers, many of whom had accompanied the deputation to the council, demonstrated their determination to preserve their town against unwelcome change by tearing down part of Wells' offending wire fence. The police intervened. About twenty of the men had their names taken. Nevertheless, many of them returned at a carefully chosen time in the evening (while the police were changing beats) and continued with the work of clearance. A much larger length of fence went down. Finding it impossible to pull its iron supports out of the ground, the men snapped them in two. Austen's shorter wooden fence was due to be next, but time had run out. Austen's fence would have to wait. It did not have to wait long.

Next day, one of the activists, Wakefield, ringing a bell like a town-crier, toured the streets in a pony and cart to announce the holding that evening of a meeting in front of the Town Hall. Public feeling was high: about a thousand people assembled. From outside the Town Hall, and as Wakefield again rang the bell, the crowd surged along St Peter's Street to the field of battle in Sandpit Lane. Wisely, the police did not try to interfere except for the taking of names.

'A long saw was now raised,' reported the *Herts Advertiser* on 19 July, 'and by means of this and other efforts brought to bear, the fence, together with its supports, was, after considerable difficulty entirely demolished.'

The work completed, the victory march followed. Led by a man carrying the long saw, the marchers returned singing along St Peter's Street to Holywell Hill where, outside Westell's house, and, further down, Hurlock's, they sang, 'For he's a jolly good fellow.' Neither councillor appeared, and the marchers re-traced their steps to the city centre before dispersing about half-past ten.

As had been knowledgeably forecast, Westell and Hurlock along with the six activists were summoned by Wells and Austen for being involved in the destruction of the fences. Wells further charged them with maliciously damaging ornamental trees. The defendants pleaded not guilty to all charges.

Public interest was considerable, and spectators filled the court to capacity on both days of the trial in August. It was during the second day that Sir Edmund Beckett's disdain became most apparent. From the height of his membership of the Church of England, he referred to Pastor Taylor, a defence witness, as a 'dissenting minister' or a 'dissenting preacher', and sneeringly described another witness, William Paul, the well known carpenter of Sandridge, as a 'farmer'. Later, he informed the court: 'We are not to be convinced by the opinion of a lot of ignorant people, who thought they had a right. It is a mere waste of time to call all these farmers and others.' But they did have a right, argued a defence barrister, and that, he said, was a good defence in the proceedings. Beckett was horrified. 'If the argument were right,' he declared as though St Albans hovered on the brink of red revolution, 'no property would be safe.'

35. *'Brummagem Joe' Chamberlain.*

For that moment, however, property was safe. The eight defendants were found guilty of destroying Wells' fence. Westell and Hurlock — 'leaders of this movement', according to Beckett — were fined £5 each; the others — 'men in somewhat inferior positions in life to town councillors' — were fined £2.10s each. Damages and costs amounted to £37 4s 6d. Failure to pay would incur a month's imprisonment. Crowhurst, Martin, Hilliard and Wakefield were found guilty of destroying Austen's fence. They, too, were fined £2.10s each, or one month, with damages and costs amounting to £39 1s 6d. Westell, Hurlock, Toms and Giddens were dismissed on the charge of destroying Austen's fence and the summonses regarding Wells' trees were dismissed for lack of evidence. Beckett took the trouble to point out that if any of the defendants were ever again convicted of a similar offence they would be liable to be imprisoned for a year, with hard labour, without the option of a fine. Appropriately, Westell and Hurlock paid their own fines and legal costs; they also contributed to a public 'Fines Fund' for the activists and Hurlock helped with their legal costs.

Pastor Taylor, too, went on fighting the good fight. 'Although some cannot afford to speak out,' he declared in a letter to the *Herts Advertiser* of 20 September 1884, 'and individuals may be for the moment silenced, a sound public opinion sooner or later asserts itself in answer to the questions which are, after all, paramount in the whole controversy, namely, Is the forcible acquisition of public land by private owners, who cannot produce a thread of title, to be winked at by the public authorities, or are the people's representatives... to resist encroachment of all kind and from every quarter whatever?'

Wells and Austen triumphantly re-erected their fences but the triumph was hollow. The battle had not ended. Complaints were made by the National Footpath Preservation Society to Sandpit Lane's Lord of the Manor, Earl Spencer, who 'most decidedly' disapproved of the encroachment. Westell, too, complained, and Earl Spencer thanked him for the part he had played.

'A deputation was therefore appointed to interview the Lord of the Manor,' an anonymous 'Old Albanian' recalled in *Memories of the Development and Growth of St Albans* (1921), 'the result being that he ordered the fence to be removed, which was done, and the open space is still in possession of the public for their use.'

The second battle of Sandpit Lane finally had been won. The first battle was fought five hundred years earlier when, during the Peasants' Revolt of 1381, Thomas de la Mare, Abbot of St Albans Abbey, granted the townsfolk a common of pasture in perpetuity — along Sandpit Lane.

# 9
# THAT VIRULENT DISEASE

*As if the inevitable risks of life were not enough.*
George Gissing: *The Town Traveller*

ARTHUR Edward Ekins enjoyed getting things done. And, as far as he was concerned, if things were worth getting done, they were worth getting done well. 'My intention,' he said confidently when chosen to be mayor of St Albans in November 1901, 'is to do the thing well.' His confidence was soon put to a fearful test: the outbreak of yet another epidemic.

Contagious epidemics were a fact of life. Despite the Public Health Act of 1848, and subsequent legislation, the danger persisted. Slums, crude sanitation and dirty drinking water assisted the spread of the diseases. For instance, in 1901, water in wells in the St Stephen's rural district of St Albans was found on analysis to be unsafe for drinking. At Wheathampstead, two-hundred-and-sixty occupants of sixty-five houses shared twenty-two earth closets, which could not be emptied. Forty children in the Sisters' Hospital — now part of St Albans City Hospital — shared the use of its only bath with all the other patients. Conditions, though, were improving. In St Albans, however, there had already been an outbreak of scarlet fever during the year; earlier, there was a typhoid fever epidemic. Diptheria, tuberculosis and, among children, diarrhoea, remained prevalent.

The impending epidemic was smallpox. Of all the epidemic diseases it long had been the most feared, the most widely diffused, the most frequent and the most deadly. Even those lucky enough to survive it were likely to be scarred by pockmarks or, as happened to the unfortunate Lady Mary Wortley Montagu in the early eighteenth century, left without eye-lashes. She had, at least, the satisfaction of introducing from Turkey inoculation against the highly contagious viral disease. There was no other defence until in 1796 Dr Edward Jenner discovered vaccination. Of the two methods of protection, vaccination was safer by far. It was made compulsory by Act of Parliament in 1853 for all newly born infants although some parents spurned it either for their children or when invited for themselves. Most, perhaps, had their reasons; every one of them, certainly, was taking a risk. For instance, middle-aged residents of St Albans in 1901 could recall at least one previous occasion when the town had been afflicted by smallpox.

A recurrence was due. Indeed, London was undergoing a severe outbreak. And the spread of the disease to St Albans was, surely, a matter of time. Fast, firm action would then be needed. Fortunately, Ekins, a retired chemist, was the right man to take charge. By temperament and training, he was equipped for the job. Born in 1852, the son of an Isle of Ely farmer, he served his apprenticeship in Cambridge. In 1874, aged twenty-two, he came to work for a chemist in Market Place, St Albans, bought the business, married, and, by dint of much study and painstaking work, achieved distinction in his profession.

36. Date plaque — A.D. 1902 — on the front wall of terrace houses in Cannon Street, St Albans.

In the 1880s, as well as becoming a director of the temperance Coffee Tavern in Market Place, he served as temporary dispenser for the St Albans Hospital and Dispensary on Holywell Hill. In 1899, two years after retiring from the business, he was elected as a Conservative member of St Albans City Council. Only two years later, his astounding energy and his popularity in the fulfilment of municipal duties prompted his colleagues unanimously to elect him as mayor. He continued to serve as the county analyst for Hertfordshire, public analyst for the borough of Luton and analyst for the Hertfordshire Agricultural Society. Admitted to life fellowships of the Chemical Society and of the Institute of Chemistry, in 1901 he was divisional secretary of the Pharmaceutical Society and a member of the council of the Society of Public Analysts. Ekins knew all that there was to know about the deadliness of smallpox. His acceptance of personal risk in tackling the outbreak revealed a stubborn bravery.

He needed to be brave. As expected, the epidemic spread from London. Within days of Ekins becoming mayor, a smallpox case was reported in Abbots Langley; more cases were reported the next month, December, in Rickmansworth and Uxbridge. In St Albans, an increase in the number of people seeking vaccination, or re-vaccination, had occurred already, and would continue to increase as the epidemic intensified. Free treatment was available. In London, so serious was the outbreak, arrangements were made for the erection of wooden sheds as emergency isolation wards at Dartford, Kent. Employed in their construction was Sidney Haycock, a carpenter, of Oster Street, St Albans. Early in the new year, 1902, he returned home as usual but complained of feeling unwell. A doctor was called, who diagnosed smallpox, and Haycock was taken by ambulance to South Mimms Isolation Hospital. The hospital had agreed to accommodate smallpox patients from St Albans as the council did not want them in the Sisters' Hospital because of the large number of patients, mainly children, suffering from scarlet fever. Haycock's wife and two children were ordered to remain at home in quarantine for a fortnight. Their house was fumigated. On 11 January, the city's residents were reassured by the *Herts Advertiser*: 'The removal of the case to a distance of several miles, combined with the steps which the local authority are taking, should render a further outbreak very improbable.'

*37. Lady Mary Wortley Montagu*

Reassurance was important. Greatly alarmed, many more people in St Albans were clamouring for vaccination. But there was a temporary shortage of vaccine. And in Hemel Hempstead, where six cases occurred, a man died of the disease. It appeared in Park Street. Henrietta King, the twenty-four-year-old wife of a railway platelayer and mother of a three-month-old child, contracted the disease while visiting her brother-in-law, Haycock, of Oster Street, before the cause of his illness had been diagnosed. Henrietta was taken to the South Mimms hospital. Her husband, their child, and the husband's sister, who lived with them, were quarantined for seventeen days after being vaccinated. Their cottage was fumigated and the bedding destroyed. A kind neighbour did the shopping — the money being transmitted through a bowl of carbolic. King's wages, £1 a week, were paid by the rural district council during his quarantine. Later in January, a case in Watford was followed by another in St Albans. The victim, an eighteen-year-old bricklayer, of Fishpool Street, was taken to South Mimms.

Ekins, who had been involved from the start of the outbreak, personally supervised the arrangements for the isolation of those infected. In February, as chairman of the city council's smallpox emergency committee, he did not hesitate to call a committee meeting on a Sunday. The occasion was the discovery that a labourer, William Clark, a former resident of the City Lodging House, Sopwell Lane, was in hospital suffering from smallpox. About thirty other people occupied the lodging house. What if some of them, or all, were infected? Could the spread of the disease be restricted to the house? How safe was the rest of St Albans? Confronted by such questions, and an alarming prospect, Ekins expected a determined response from his committee. The members obliged. At once, the lodging house was closed. The premises and bedding were fumigated. The occupants were placed in quarantine. Some who had not been vaccinated, accepted it immediately; remarkably, most refused. And because none of them was allowed to go out to work, the city council granted individual allowances equal to twelve-and-a-half-pence a day. Relays of police kept watch outside to prevent anybody leaving or entering.

*38. Arthur Ekins*

For a while, the danger seemed to have passed. No further cases were reported. The rigorous measures could, perhaps, be accounted successful. In fact, the outbreak had been contained, not eradicated. One after the other, the lodging house landlady, Ruth Skinner, her husband, Thomas, and two of their lodgers, William Harris and John Bertram, were found to be infected. Thomas Skinner died four days after being admitted to hospital. The others recovered. In early March, three more lodgers, John Toms, Samuel Taylor and Joseph Brandon, developed a mild form of the disease. They were taken to an emergency isolation hut in the grounds of St Albans Workhouse (adjacent to the Sisters' Hospital) where a tramp suspected of smallpox had been detained after seeking shelter. He died six days later and was buried without delay at night. Neither his death nor time of burial aroused comment. After all, he was a pauper. But what about John Bertram? He had been living at the City Lodging House although lacking any means of his own. Was he a pauper, too? The answer mattered financially. If destitute, he was chargeable to the workhouse Board of Guardians; if not destitute, he was the responsibility of the city council.

Separately and at length the board and the council discussed the matter. The board's vice-chairman, the Rev Henry Taylor, a veteran of the battle of Sandpit Lane, said the whole thing turned on the definition of destitution. If a patient were unable to supply himself with food, medical attendance and medical nursing, that person was destitute. Richard Samuel, a member of the board, contended that Bertram did not qualify because 'another authority' — the city council — had designated him a pauper. Consequently, the whole expense should fall upon the council. Ekins, too, was a board member, and said that the council thought that Bertram was undoubtedly a pauper. 'I have had a great deal to do with this matter,' he explained, 'and the town council has had two special meetings with regard to it.' He assured a subsequent meeting of the board that the council would not quibble about paying its share of the expenses in dealing with the outbreak. Bertram, whose views are not known, was eventually acknowledged to be a pauper.

*39. The Sisters' Hospital, 1893, is now part of St Albans City Hospital*

'It will be good news to many of the citizens of St Albans,' said the *Herts Advertiser* on 8 March, 'that the City Lodging House, which was the chief centre of the outbreak in our city, is no longer, in the medical opinion, a source of danger. On Thursday, [6 March] the quarantine order was removed and police supervision withdrawn, the inmates, having all been medically examined and deemed to be free from any trace of the disease, were released, having been first thoroughly disinfected and new clothes having been supplied by the Corporation.' A week later, 15 March, the newspaper reported that no fewer than seven hundred residents had obtained free vaccination since the beginning of the year. 'Considerable numbers' were said still to be seeking re-vaccination.

Their concern was understandable. Another outbreak, entirely localised, occurred at Easter. The first victim, a Mrs Wells, of Boundary Road, was taken to the isolation hut where on Good Friday, 28 March, her six-year-old daughter, Eliza, was admitted with the disease. The same day, Mary Smith, aged eight, of Culver Road, was found to have contracted it. She died that night. On Easter Sunday another eight-year-old girl, of Walton Street, was notified as suffering from smallpox and on Tuesday, Winifred Stone, aged three, of Heath Road, was taken to the isolation hut. As usual, the families were quarantined, their houses fumigated and disinfected. Two more children in the district became mildly infected but neither of them, nor any of the other sick children, died. The only other smallpox case during April was that of a carter, William Davis, of Fishpool Street, who was taken to the isolation hut. His wife and three children were quarantined in their swiftly disinfected home. In June, two working men, both staying at a public house in Fishpool Street, became victims of the disease. One of them died, and the landlady, too, fell ill but recovered. They were the last cases. It was midsummer. And of greater importance than the cold wet weather was the fact that the smallpox outbreak in St Albans had ended. More widely, its days in Great Britain were numbered. Smallpox was being eradicated.

Ten years later, in March 1912, the *Herts Advertiser* found it necessary to remind readers of how Ekins had tackled the smallpox outbreak despite the risk of endangering his own health. The article continued: 'He had the reward, however, of knowing that by reason of the promptitude with which the outbreak was taken in hand the city was protected from any considerable spread of that virulent disease.' Ekins had died suddenly at his home in Upper Lattimore Road. He was sixty.

# 10
# FESTIVAL OF HISTORY

*Thus in the tranquil town of St Albans, crucial issues of today make themselves felt during celebrations of an event that happened six-hundred years ago.*

Editorial: *Herts Advertiser*

THE six-hundredth anniversary of the Peasants' Revolt was commemorated widely throughout England during 1981. Naturally, the commemoration varied from place to place. There were public meetings. Books, booklets or propagandist picture postcards were issued in places as different as Colchester, Kettering and Brighton. Daily newspapers and specialist journals carried articles. The BBC broadcast a radio play and, a week later, a documentary. But only in one place, St Albans, were the commemorative events so numerous, so varied, so extensive. They lasted from March to July. They involved people and organisations, independently or in association, ranging from traders, academics and folk singers to churches, trade unions and schools. Civically, by any reckoning, it was an unprecedented popular commemoration.

It would have been disgraceful had it been otherwise. The people of St Albans took an active, passionate part in the revolt of 1381. They were not onlookers, indifferent to its outcome, as they probably were some eighty years later when squalid dynastic wars brought savagery to the streets of the town. In 1381, people of St Albans whole-heartedly joined up with their counterparts throughout south-east England to fight against oppression. The uprising's brutal suppression and the execution of its leaders, including that of the local hero, William Grindcobbe,

*40. Deidre Roger's poster traces the causes and course of the Peasants' Revolt in St Albans*

failed to extinguish the flame of freedom. Successive generations were inspired by the uprising to take up the torch again and again. In 1981 its light sparkled in various eyes.

Among them were those of Edwin Hudson (1917 –90). For many years a city councillor, it was at his prompting in the summer of 1980 that St Albans Constituency Labour Party agreed to organise public activities to mark the six-hundredth anniversary. Of course, the uprising had demanded commemoration. It was too historic an occasion to neglect. Indeed, other organisations in St Albans were of a similar opinion. In different ways, the past mattered. And might not the past have implications for the present? A committee was formed. Preparations began immediately. Offers of help, ideas and plans multiplied.

In October 1980, two historians, Alan Hooper and Graham Pechey, both of St Albans, and lecturers at Hatfield Polytechnic, wrote to the *St Albans Review*.

Reminding readers of the anniversary's approach, they urged 'interested parties of all kinds . . . to take an initiative of some description' and invited co-operation. The outcome was the formation of a small group. As well as the two lecturers, the group included the historian Geoff Dunk, a street theatre organiser and a Quaker. They decided to try to arrange a conference. Quickly, thanks to the co-operation of journalists, the columns of the local press filled with reports and photographs relating to the events: that unflagging publicity was essential to the commemoration's popularity.

Geoff Dunk raised the curtain. In his *Review* weekly

*41. Edwin Hudson*

local history article of 16 October 1980 he described how the great gateway of St Albans Abbey was entered by the rebels. Three months later, in January 1981, he devoted his column to the causes of the uprising and returned to the theme in subsequent articles. Meanwhile, the Labour Party had announced that Donald Soper, the Methodist minister and peer, would be speaking at a public commemorative meeting in the Town Hall in June. Already, preparations had been made by Hertfordshire Local History Council and Hertfordshire Library Service jointly to publish *The Peasants' Revolt in Hertfordshire, 1381: the Rising and its Background*. Along with general surveys, it promised extracts from a previously untranslated history of the uprising by the nineteenth-century French historian, André Réville. By the early spring of 1981, street events, exhibitions, lectures and the conference had been planned. More events occurred spontaneously during the commemorative summer.

The first event was on 12 March at St Albans Labour Party headquarters in Alma Road when Stanley Robertson, the author of a musical play about the revolt, gave an illustrated talk. In April, the Party published an illustrated leaflet, selling at ten pence a copy, which listed all the announced events. It also put on sale, at £2 each, commemorative T-shirts. The word 'Revolt' dominated the chest; above, smaller, was 'Peasants', and, below, '1381 –1981'. It proved to be popular.

Centrally, at the city's medieval Clock Tower, an historical display was organised by St Albans and Hertfordshire Architectural and Archaeological Society. Later, a pictorial exhibition went on display for a week at Harpenden Library. *The Medieval Borough Boundary of St Albans*, a Civic Society lecture on the boundary's significance in the uprising, was given at the Town Hall.

*42. A commemorative pottery mug made in St Albans.*

May began with St Albans Folk Music Club performing A Little Liberty, the uprising's story in words and music, at *The Goat* public house, Sopwell Lane. The club room filled rapidly and, because many people had to be turned away, the show was repeated in July. The club also repeated it at a commemorative celebration at Blackheath where, in 1381, the rebels had assembled before entering London triumphantly.

A large, coloured poster, privately produced, depicted the causes and course of the uprising. Costing fifty pence a copy, it went on sale at the city museums and a bookshop. Outline copies were printed for children to colour. The poster was the work of an artist, Deirdre Rogers, who taught at Loreto College, St Albans. Nearby, the Church of SS Alban and Stephen, linking the peasants of the past with those of the day, displayed a photographic exhibition on world rural poverty. But it was at the Abbey and at a rally outside in Abbey Orchard that the largest and most rowdy commemorative events occurred.

The National Union of Agricultural and Allied Workers had arranged with the Dean of St Albans, the Very Rev Dr Peter Moore — a former member of the union — to hold a service of commemoration and thanksgiving in the Abbey on Sunday, 31 May. Excerpts were sung from an opera, *Wat Tyler*, by the composer Alan Bush, of Radlett. The union's general secretary, Jack Boddy, gave the address. Prayers were led by the Dean. Crowding the Abbey were union members from all over the country. With their banners flying, preceded by bands, they had marched to the Abbey from Bernard's Heath, along St Peter's Street, pausing in Upper Dagnall Street to place wreaths near the commemorative plaque outside the old Moot Hall where Grindcobbe and other leaders were tried. Later, a platter specially commissioned by the union to celebrate the uprising was presented to the Dean; another had been donated to the City Museum.

The rowdiness was at the rally in Abbey Orchard. Speaking at it was the Labour Party leader, Michael Foot. A dozen hecklers, some waving placards, interrupted his speech to protest about Northern Ireland. Between chanting 'Troops out,' they jeered and heckled until the rally ended. Another group of protesters, though less noisy, consisted of St Albans campaigners for nuclear disarmament. 'As is so often the case in St Albans,' commented the *Herts Advertiser* editorial of 5 June (from which the epigraph to this chapter is taken), 'things didn't go quite so smoothly as planned.'

43. *Young Liberals march with the agricultural workers and others along St Peter's Street, St Albans.*

Surprisingly, the comment soon was verified. St Albans Co-operative Society's political group had organised a competition for children to enter pictures with 'revolt' as the theme. The entries were exhibited in the Town Hall, and the mayor, Kenneth Jenkins, was invited to present the prizes. He declined. 'There is enough conflict in the world today,' he told the organisers, 'be it in Northern Ireland or elsewhere, without encouraging children to spend their leisure time depicting the theme of revolt.'

Nothing clouded the remaining events. There was something for everyone: commemorative mugs produced by a potter, Chris Buras, at St Albans Pottery in Spicer Street; a pictorial display in a window of W.H. Smith & Son's shop, which occupies the Moot Hall; a pictorial display at St Albans Central Library; Verulamium Museum's mobile exhibition in a caravan at St Albans and Harpenden; a lecture in the Abbey Gateway; *Robin Hood, Rogues and Rebels*, a talk by the author Robert Leeson to children in St Albans Central Library; Morris dancers from Yorkshire joining with those of the city's Cottonmill Clog Morris at displays in St Albans, Colney Heath, Lemsford and Tyttenhanger Green; Lord Soper delivering his lecture, and the following week, on 24 June, the journalist Paul Foot, and Reg Groves, the author of the agricultural workers' union history, addressing a public meeting arranged by St Albans Trades Council at the Town Hall.

Bringing the month's busy programme to a spectacular close were performances at the Abbey of *This Impatient Nettle*, a dramatisation of the events leading

*44. The marchers were led by Jack Boddy, general secretary of the National Union of Agricultural and Allied Workers, Joan Maynard M.P., and Norman Willis, deputy general secretary of the Trades Union Congress.*

up to the revolt. Commissioned by the Fraternity of Friends of St Albans Abbey, its author, Philip Gillmor, directed and took part in the production with actors belonging to the Company of Ten from the Abbey Theatre, St Albans.

A four-mile walk around the city's medieval boundary, organised by St Albans District Council, heralded the events of July. The walkers, following in the footsteps of fourteenth-century burgesses, were re-creating the assertive custom of Beating the Bounds.

45. *Farmworkers' badge*

For some, the highlight of the events was the day-long commemorative conference, *The Rising of 1381*, at St Albans School on 18 July. Opened by the scrupulous mayor, Kenneth Jenkins, and with patrons such as the Bishop of St Albans, the Rt Rev John Taylor, it attracted two hundred participants to hear and discuss lectures by five distinguished historians: Rodney Hilton, speaking on *Peasants, Artisans and Others*; Eileen Roberts: *The Architecture of Conflict*; Arthur Jones: *The Rising in St Albans*; Rosamund Faith: *Rights, Memories and Traditions*; and J.J. Smith, of the Royal Commission on Historic Monuments, on the architecture of the period.

Appropriately, the wheel of events came full-circle at the Abbey. There, on the evening of 18 July, where six-hundred years earlier the rebels had confronted Abbot Thomas de la Mare, a lecture, *The Peasants' Revolt and the Christian Faith Today*, was given by Edwin Hudson. In a sentence central to his faith and to his politics he invoked the ideal of the peasants' Great Fellowship: 'The authority of society to command the respect and love of its members has to be authenticated by its care and its justice towards those whose adherence it is demanding.' Calmly, he was issuing a challenge: that the link between past and present was real and relevant; that the commemoration should not be regarded as an exercise in antiquarian fossicking but as an inspiration.

After all, an outstanding act in the drama of the English people's democratic endeavour had been commemorated and it had amounted to more than an episode in a pageant. The total achievement in St Albans was remarkable and rare: a summer-long festival of history.

# SOURCES

STANDARD sources, such as *The Dictionary of National Biography*, are not listed; neither are works mentioned in the text. Newspapers and journals consulted include the *Herts Advertiser, Hertfordshire Countryside, Hertfordshire Past & Present, Herts Mercury, Illustrated London News, Punch, The Quiver, St Albans and Harpenden Observer, St Albans Review* and *The Strand Magazine* as well as various *Transactions* of the St Albans and Hertfordshire Architectural and Archaeological Society.

    Anon., *Sketches of Eminent Primitive Methodists*, London, 1872.

    Ashdown, Charles, *St Albans Historical and Picturesque*, London, 1893. Barratt,

    D.W., *Sketches of Church Life*, London, 1902.

    Chapman, R.M., ed., *Jane Austen's Letters*, London, sec.ed. 1952.

    Chambers, R., ed., *The Book of Days*, London, 1886.

    Deacon, Audrey, and Walne, Peter, eds., *Cussans, John Edwin, A Professional Hertfordshire Tramp*, Hertfordshire Record Society, 1987.

    Dryden, John, *Poems and Fables*, ed. James Kinsley, London, 1958.

    Garvin, J.L., *Life of Joseph Chamberlain*, London, 1932.

    Gibbs, A.E., *The Corporation Records of St Albans*, St Albans, 1890.

    Giles, E., and Thrale, W., *Historic Sandridge*, St Albans, 1952. Groves, Reg, *Sharpen the Sickle: History of the Agricultural Workers' Union*, London, 1949.

    Hebditch, Felicity, *J.H. Buckingham: A Window on Victorian St Albans*, St Albans, 1988.

    Hibberd, Shirley, *The Fern Garden*, London, 1869.

    Jones-Baker, Doris, ed., *Hertfordshire in History*, Hertfordshire Local History Council, 1991.

    King, Norah, *The Grimstons of Gorhambury*, Chichester, 1983.

    Kingston, Alfred, *Herts during the Great Civil War*, London, 1894.

Lefevre, George, *Commons, Forests and Footpaths*, London, 1910.
Marlow, Joyce, *The Tolpuddle Martyrs*, London, 1971.
Oliver, Anthony, *The Victorian Staffordshire Figure*, London, 1971.
Parker, Meryl, ed., *All My Wordly Goods*, Bricket Wood Society, 1991.
Rook, Tony, *A History of Hertfordshire*, Chichester, 1984.
Rogers, James, ed., *Speeches of John Bright*, London, 1869.
Scott, Dom Geoffrey, *St Alban Roe OSB*, St Albans, 1991.
Trevelyan, G.M., *Garibaldi and the Making of Italy*, London, 1911.
Urwick, William, *Nonconformity in Hertfordshire*, London, 1884.

# INDEX

Abbey, and Abbey Church of, St Albans, 1, 3, 5, 6, 9, 16, 19, 21, 30, 35, 54, 56, 61, 70–74
Abbey Theatre, 73
Abbots Langley, 64
Agricultural Labourers' Union, 47; Society, Herts., 63; Workers', Union of, 72
Albert Street, 38
Alderman, H.M., 37
Allen, Joseph, 48
Alma Road, 71
Anabaptists, 22,
Anne, Queen of England, 4
America, South, 39; United States of, 52
Archaeological Society, 37, 71
Arch, Joseph, 47
Ashton, Nelson, 44
Austen, Frederick, 55–57, 61–62
Austen, Rev George, 29
Austen, Jane, 29
Australia, 46
Avenue Road, 55

Babbe, William, 15
Bacon, Sir Francis, Lord Verulam, 27
Baptists, 17, 57
Beckett, Sir Edmund, Lord Grimthorpe, 54, 60, 61
Bedford, 21
Benedictines, 5, 8, 9
Benskin's, 42, 44
Berchmore, Thomas, 15
Bernard's Heath, 51, 54, 72
Bertram, John, 65
Block, Gerard, 44
Boddy, Jack, 72
Boundary Road, 67
Brandon, Joseph, 66
Bright, John, 41
B.B.C., 68
Brown, Alice, 44

Browne, John, 15
Buckingham, John Henry, 33, 34
Buckinghamshire, 31, 47
Bunyan, John, 21
Buras, Chris, 73
Bury St Edmunds, 3
Bush, Alan, 72
Butler, William, 51


Cambridge, 3, 63
Camm, Dom Bede, 8
Catholics, 3–5, 7, 8, 32
Challoner, Richard, 8
Chamberlain, Joseph, 56
Charles I, King of England, 5, 6, 10–12, 15
Charles II, King of England, 16, 18, 20
Chauncy, Sir Henry, 20
Chemical Society, 63
Chemistry, Institute of, 63
Christ Church, 30, 32, 33, 36, 37
City Lodging House, 65–67
City Museum, 72
Civic Society, 71
Clark, William, 65
Clock Tower, 33–35, 71
Cobden, Richard, 41
Coffee Tavern, 63
Coleman Green, 21
College Street, 23
Collegium Insanorum, 23, 24
Colney Heath, 51, 73
Company of Ten, 74
Commons, House of, 5, 13, 20, 52, 56
Congregationalist, 17, 21, 22
Co-operative Society, 72
Conservative, 63
Corn Exchange, 39, 52, 58
Corn Laws, 40, 41, 50
Cotton, Nathaniel, 23–29
Cotton, Rev Nathaniel, 29

# INDEX

Council, St Albans, 33, 34, 63, 74
Cowper, William, 23, 24, 28
Cricket Club, Hertfordshire County, 56
Cromwell, Oliver, 11, 41
Crosby, Edward, 20, 21
Crowhurst, Edgar, 54, 61
Culver Road, 67
Cussans, Edwin, 49

'David', 3–5, 7
Dartford, Kent, 64
Davis, William, 67
Davys, Rev Canon Owen William, 48, 49
Dieulouard, 5
Douai, 4, 5, 8
Dryden, John, 11, 17, 18
Dunk, Geoff, 9, 70
Dunstable, 23

Edgehill, 12
Ekins, Arthur Edward, 62–67
Ellicot, Dr, 49
England, Church of, 4, 9, 11, 15–19, 32, 33
Everett, Hannah, 26, 29

Faith, Rosamund, 74
Fishpool Street, 3, 65, 67
Fleet prison, 6
Fleur de Lys public house, 42
Folk Music Club, 71
France, 39
Foot, Michael, 72
Foot, Paul, 73
Footpath Preservation Society, National, 61

Garibaldi, Giuseppe, 39–42, 44
Garibaldi public house, 38, 40–42, 44, 50
Garnett, R.S., 40
Gateway, Abbey, 3, 6, 73
George Street, 35
Giddens, William, 54, 61
Gillmor, Philip, 73

Goat public house, 42, 171
Gondomar, Count of, 5
Gorhambury, 20
Graham, Kenneth, 40
Grey, Edwin, 45
Grimston, Sir Harbottle, 20, 21
Grindcobbe, William, 68, 72
Groves, Reg, 73

Halsey, Thomas, 15
Hampshire, 28
Hare, John, 15
Harpenden, 9, 45, 50, 51, 71, 73
Harris, William, 65
Harrow public house, 42
Hatfield, 46
Hatfield Polytechnic, 69
Hatfield Road, 42
Haworth, Rev William, 18–20, 22
Haycock, Sidney, 64
Heath Road, 67
Hemel Hempstead, 64
Henrietta Maria, Queen of England, 5
Henry VIII, King of England, 3
Hertford, 21, 22
Hertfordshire, 12–14, 17, 18, 40, 44–47, 49, 63, 70; Library Service, 70; Local History Council, 70
Hibbert, Eliza, 44
Hibbert, Henry, 42, 44
High Street, 33–35
Hill Street, 43
Hilliard, William, 54, 61
Hilton, Rodney, 74
Holywell Hill, 3, 12, 55, 60, 61, 63
Hooper, Alan, 69
Hospital, St Albans, 33, 63
Hudson, Edwin, 69, 74
Hume, Cardinal Basil, 9
Humphrey, John, 15
Hurlock, William, 37, 54–61

Ireland, 41, 72
Iron Room, 40
Italy, 38–40

# INDEX

Iver, Bucks, 31

James I, King of England, 4, 5
Jarrow-on-Tyne, 43
Jenkins, Kenneth, 72, 74
Jenner, Dr Edward, 63
Jones, Arthur, 74

King, Henrietta, 64

Labour Party, 69–72
Lattimore, Ann Eliza, 41
Lattimore, Charles Higby, 40, 41, 50
Lattimore Road, 32, 41
Leeson, Robert, 73
Lemsford, 73
Lemsford Road, 44, 53
Leyden, 23
Liberals, 41, 55, 56
Library, Central, St Albans, 73
Licensed Victuallers', 42
Liddell, Rev Canon Edward, 42, 43
Lloyd, John, 42
London, 5, 6, 12, 23, 26, 32, 33, 38, 40, 55, 63, 64
London Road, 30
Loreto College, 71
Loveless, George, 46
Lower Dagnall Street, 23, 24
Lucy, Charles, 40
Luton, 63

Mare, Abbot Thomas de la, 61, 74
Market Place, 30, 33, 35, 56, 58, 63
Martin, pedler, 54, 61
Martin, Thomas, 42
Mason, Frederick, 2, 54
Massachusetts, 11
Methodists, 70; Primitive, 47
Montagu, Lady Mary Wortley, 62
Moore, Very Rev Dr Peter, 72
Morris dancers: Yorkshire, 73; Cottonmill, 73
Moot Hall, 72, 73

Nelson, Lord Horatio, 41
Netherlands, Spanish, 4
Neve, William, 10
Newgate prison, 7
Nomansland Common, 47
Nottingham, 12

Oddfellows, Loyal Alban Lodge of, 42
Old Bailey, 7, 20, 21
Old London Road, 335
Oster Street, 64

Park Street, 64
Parliament, 6, 7, 10–15, 18, 20, 32, 38, 56
Paul, William, 48, 51, 60
Peasants' Revolt, 2, 61, 68, 70, 74
Pechey, Graham, 69
Pembroke, Ann, 24, 29
Pharmaceutical Society, 63
Presbyterians, 17, 22
Protestants, 5, 16, 18
Public Analysts, Society of, 64
Puritans, 5, 6, 16, 17, 20

Quakers, 17, 22, 70

Radlett, 72
Railway station, 54, 55
Raphael, Alexander, 32
Ratcliffe, Timothy, 20, 21
Red Lion public house, 42
Reformer beer house, 42
Revillé, André, 70
Reynolds, Rev Thomas, 7
Rickmansworth, 64
Roberts, Eileen, 74
Robertson, Stanley, 71
Roe, St Alban (Bartholomew), 3–9, 15
Rogers, Deirdre, 71
Rolfe, Williams, 15
Royal British Legion, 32

St Alban, 5, 9
St Albans Pottery, 73

# INDEX

SS Alban & Stephen Church, 71
St Helen's Church, Wheathampstead, 49
St Peter's Church, 18, 19, 22, 24, 29–31, 37
St Peter's Park, 54, 55
St Peter's Street, 3, 24, 27, 34, 59, 60, 72
St Stephen's parish, 14, 5;
 rural district, 62
Samuel, Richard, 66
Sandpit Lane, 53–55, 58, 59, 61, 66
Sandridge, 46, 48, 51, 60
Scott, Dom Geoffrey, 9
Scott, Sir Gilbert, 30, 33–35, 37
Shenley, 13
Sisters' Hospital, 62, 64, 66
Skinner, Thomas & Ruth, 65
Smallpox, 62–67
Smiles, Samuel, 45
Smith, Councillor, 57
Smith, Rev Henry, 37
Smith, J.J., 74
Smith, Mary, 67
Smith, W.H. & Son, 73
Soper, Lord Donald, 70, 73
Sopwell House, 31, 37
Sopwell Lane, 65, 71
Southampton, 40
South Mimms Isolation Hospital, 64, 65
Spencer, Earl, 61
Spicer Street, 73
Stone, Winifred, 67
Stonecross, 53
Strong, Edward, 31

Taylor, Rev Henry, 57–61, 66
Taylor, Rt Rev John, Bishop, 74
Taylor, Samuel, 66
Thompson, Flora, 49
Thursby, Northants., 29
Timperon, Arthur, 31
Timperon, Joseph & Anne, 31, 37
Tolpuddle Martyrs, 46
Toms, Edwin, 54, 56
Toms, John, 66
Town Hall, 34, 54, 59, 70–72

Townsend, John, 16–22
Turkey, 63
Turrill, Charles & Elizabeth, 19
Tyburn, 7
Tyler, Wat, 72
Tyttenhanger Green, 73

Upper Dagnall Streeet, 72
Upper Lattimore Road, 67
Uxbridge, 64

Ver, river, 31
Verulam Golf Club, 37
Verulam Road, 30, 32, 35, 40, 42
Verulamium Museum, 73
Victoria Square, 30, 33, 37
Victoria Street, 57, 58

Wakefield, Harry, 54, 59, 61
Walmsley, Sir Joshua, 40, 41
Walton Street, 67
Watford, 32, 38, 42, 65
Watson's Walk, 44
Wells, Eliza, 67
Wells, H.G., 40
Wells, John, 55–57, 59, 60, 61
Wells, Mrs, 67
Welwyn, 24
Westell, William, 54–58, 60, 61
Westell, William Percival, 44
West Indies, 3
Wheathampstead, 40, 41, 48–50, 62
White Lion public house, 42
Wiles, Edward, 33
Wingate, Edward,, 13
Winter, Holmes, 43
Wooden Room, 33, 37
Workhouse, 43, 66
Worley, Henry Thomas, 31
Worley, Isabella, 30–37
Worley Road, 36
Wren, Sir Christopher, 31

Young, Rev Edward, 24